INSIGHT COMPACT GUIDE

IBIZA

Compact [illegible] ...ate quick-reference guide to [illegible] island and its smaller neighbour Formentera. It tells you everything you need to know about the islands' attractions, from the alleyways of Eivissa to the bright lights of Sant Antoni, and the rural charms of the interior to the beautiful, varied coast.

This is one of 120 Compact Guides, which combine the interests and enthusiasms of two of the world's best known information providers: Insight Guides, whose titles have set the standard for visual travel guides since 1970, and Discovery Channel, the world's premier source of nonfiction television programming.

Star Attractions

An instant reference to some of Ibiza's top attractions to help you set your priorities.

Eivissa p17

Fishing quarter p18

Portal de Ses Taules p21

Es Cub[illegible]

Sant Antoni p40

Església de Sant Miquel p43

Benirrás p44

Xarraca p47

Jesús Church p50

Folk dancer

Sant Ferran p56

Contents

Ibiza

Introduction

Ibiza – White Island of Fun **5**
Historical Highlights **12**

Places

Route 1: Eivissa **16**
Route 2: Hotel skylines and bird sanctuaries: Eivissa – Ses Figuertes – Sant Jordi de Ses Salines – Ses Salines **29**
Route 3: The southwest: Eivissa – Sa Caleta – Sant Josep de Sa Talaia – Cala d'Hort – Sant Agustí d'Es Vedra **33**
Route 4: A favourite excursion: Eivissa – Sant Rafel de Sa Creu – Santa Agnès de Corona – Sant Antoni de Portmany **38**
Route 5: The quiet side: Eivissa – Sant Miquel de Balansat – Sant Mateu d'Aubarca – Santa Gertrudis de Fruitera **42**
Route 6: Harmony in contrast: Eivissa – Sant Llorenç de Balàfia – Sant Joan de Lab[illegible] Sant Vicenç – Es Cuiram **46**
Rout[illegible] [illegible]ssa – Talamanca – Cala Llonga– [illegible]anar – Sant Carles de Peralta **49**
Route 8: [illegible]ormentera: [illegible]ina – Ses Illetes – Es Pujols – Sant Ferran de ses Roq[illegible]es – Platja de Migjorn – El Pilar – Sant Francesç Xavier – Cap de Barbària **53**

Culture

Art and Architecture **61**
Music and Dance **62**
Festivals and F[illegible]lklore **63**

Leisure

Food and Drink **65**
Nightlife **68**
Active Holidays **69**

Practical Information

Getting There **71**
Getting Around **72**
Facts for the Visitor **73**
Accommodation **76**

Index **80**

Ibiza – White Island of Fun

Opposite: Sun-seekers rewarded

Ibiza has a special attraction all its own. The mountains are not as high or dramatic as those on the west coast of Mallorca; instead, its broad valleys are surrounded by relatively flat, rounded hills. As the summer progresses, the luxuriant green vegetation of springtime dries into parched brown fields, which only go briefly green after one of the rare rain showers. Away from the dry, green pine forests, the soil is hard and rocky with extensive salt flats in the south. Nevertheless, the small island of Ibiza exerts a gentle yet powerful attraction – and always ends up delighting and captivating its visitors.

The island's beauty is the result of a combination of several relatively unspectacular details: centuries-old walls protecting terraced fields from erosion; remote inland farms (*fincas*) blending harmoniously into the landscape; orchards and terraces covering slopes beside dried-up mountain streams; and the sparkling Mediterranean lapping against the rocky coastline, sandy coves and wide southern bays. All these details blend together to form a landscape that has an unforgettable charm.

The charm is in the detail: stone walls near Sant Joan

Ever since the1960s, Ibiza has been a mecca for young people seeking an alternative way of life. But the Bohemian lifestyles of the past, so elegantly recreated in novels by the likes of John Banville, no longer make the headlines, rather the nightclub and disco invasion of the 18–30s age group. Ibiza has become the rave capital of Europe. And the resort of Sant Antoni (San Antonio), with its British dance culture imports, is undoubtedly the centre of the action. But that is only a fraction of Ibiza; non-clubbers can equally enj[illegible] parts of the island by night or day in relative peace and, in some spots, seclusion.

Nightlife in Eivissa

In contrast, Ibiza's sister island of Formentera is far more peaceful – full of wind, sand and silence. It is mostly flat and therefore absolutely perfect for cycling around, and is just the place for a really relaxing holiday.

Position and size

The collective name *Pitiuses* applies to the islands of Ibiza, Formentera and the small rocky islands around them (Sa Conillera, Illa d'es Bosc, S'Espartar, Es Vedrà, Es Vedranell, S'Espalmador, S'Espardell, Tagomago and a host of other even smaller ones), and probably derives from the ancient Greek word *pityussai*. The Roman naturalist and geographer Pliny the Elder traced the word back to mean thick pine forests.

Ibiza and Formentera form part of the Balearic archipelago which extends away from the east coast of Spain in the western Mediterranean. Mallorca, the largest of the Balearic Islands, is only 80km (50 miles) away from Ibiza; Denia, the nearest harbour on the Spanish mainland, is only around 90km (56 miles) distant. Even the coast of North Africa is a mere 180km (110 miles) away – the same distance as Barcelona, capital of Catalonia. This strategically favourable position made Ibiza and Formentera into desirable military bases for centuries.

A flat stretch

Of the total surface area of the islands – roughly 645 sq km (250 sq miles) – Ibiza takes up 568 sq km (220 sq miles) and Formentera 82 sq km (31 sq miles). Ibiza's 210-km (130-mile) long coastline has only very few naturally sandy beaches, almost all of which lie in the south. The rest of the coast consists of slopes of rock or scree, interspersed by tiny *calas* or bays. In contrast, almost half of Formentera's 60km (37 miles) of coastline consists of long, sandy beaches.

In the hills near Sant Vincenç

Size apart, the most obvious difference between the two islands is geographical. Formentera is largely flat, and its only elevation, La Mola (192m/630ft above sea level), is actually a high plateau; whereas any tour across Ibiza is full of ups and downs. Wherever you're headed in Ibiza, ..ll will certainly obstruct the view at first, except for very close to Eivissa, the island's capital, where the fertile plain of Es Pla de Vila extends from its gates. But these elevations are rather modest. Sa Talaia (also known as Sa Talaissa), the highest mountain on Ibiza, located in the southern Serra de Sant Josep, is only 475m (1,560ft) high (the mountains on the west coast of Mallorca reach elevations of 1,100m/3 600ft in contrast).

To the north, the highest point in the massif known as the Serra de Sant Vincenç is the Puig des Fornas (410m/1,345ft), while there are lower ranges to the east surrounding wide valleys such as the fertile Pla d'Atzaro. In the northwest, Es Amunts extend for more than 160sq km

Es Codolar beach near Sa Caleta

(61 sq miles), and culminate in the rolling Es Camp Vell (398m/1,300ft).

Thick pine forests with almost impenetrable undergrowth still cover the mountain ranges today, even though many of the southern slopes have now been terraced. Farmers used to till their own small plots of hard and stony ground here until a few years ago. Most of the arable land is in the valleys, however, and is often criss-crossed by wild mountain streams known as *torrents*. Until the 1960s, these were full of water throughout the winter months. After many years of drought, however, during which the Riu de Santa Eulària, Ibiza's only river, dried up completely, the streams have all become subterranean.

Climate and when to go

Per Sant Bartomeu, tronades sentireu. If the prediction of thunder and rain on St Bartholomew's Day (24 August) fails to come true, the first rain is supposed to fall on 29 September. If it fails to arrive even then, the farmers on Ibiza usually lose all hope that the dried-up soil will be able to accommodate any seedlings during the normally rainy months of October, November and March.

An overcast sky or threatening-looking clouds are no guarantee of rain on Ibiza, and still less so on Formentera. Over the last few years, the islands' low elevation and the winds that tend to suddenly clear the sky of clouds have halved the statistical annual average of 76 rainy days. In fact Ibiza and Formentera, with their subtropical Mediterranean climate, get sunshine virtually all the time.

During July and August the temperatures rise to over 35°C (95°F) and drop no lower than 25°C (77°F) at night. Even in winter the daytime temperatures stay around 15°C (59°F) due to the sunshine, and on cooler days they fall to a mere 12°C (53°F). Frost sometimes makes a brief appearance early in the morning during January, but is soon melted by the first rays of sun.

The two islands thus have a very pleasant climate all year round, and can be visited for a holiday at any time. The best period for bathing in the sea is from June to October, and the other months are more suitable for getting to know the islands properly because there are less tourists around. The moderate temperatures then are also ideal for long hiking trips or cycling tours – during almond blossom time in January, for instance, or between February and April when the meadows bloom.

Cala Boix

Clear water off Cala Comte

Nature and environment

In 1991, the government of the Balearic Islands passed the controversial environmental protection law called the *Ley de Espacios Naturales* (LEN), aimed at preventing an uncontrolled spread of construction across the islands as well as protecting such relatively unspoilt rural areas as Es Amunts, Ses Clots d'Aubarca, Corona and Ses Salines. Environmental studies have shown that the existing holiday villages are close to taking up too much room and are a strain on resources.

Ses Salines

Since then, Ibiza and Formentera have ensured that two regions have been totally protected: the salt flats (*salinas*) on Ibiza, including the neighbouring areas of Sal Rossa and Corb Mari (1,140 hectares/2,815 acres), and the salt flats of Formentera (885 hectares/2,200 acres). All construction activity is forbidden here. An uncontrolled increase in mass tourism would make the groundwater level sink still further beneath its already alarmingly low levels. Studies have shown that seawater and sewage treatment plants could alleviate this problem to some extent but not solve it, because recycled water has been deemed not suitable for all purposes.

Since the mid-1980s, environmentalists on the two islands have fought hard and confidently for the preservation of the local flora and fauna, particularly for sheltered nesting sites for the numerous birds of passage, many of which come to the salt flats.

Sabina tree near Benirrás

The higher, forested regions on Ibiza consist mainly of Aleppo pine and Phoenician juniper (*sabina*). The undergrowth is full of rock roses, rosemary, thyme, gorse and mint, as well as numerous protected species of orchid. Falcons and other birds of prey nest here, and the forests are also home to the – nowadays extremely rare – North African genet, a wild cat brought to the island by the Moors. Screech owls and barn owls make their nests inside the hollowed-out carob trees. A common sight – also in houses – is the gecko, a type of lizard with a long tongue for catching insects. It should really be made into the heraldic animal of Formentera, and has been a protected species ever since a foreigner unsuccessfully attempted to export it. The lizards on Ibiza are smaller, and don't have the same attractive blue and green colours as the ones on Formentera.

The hoopoe (known to the locals as *puput* or *mensajero*) is a common bird in rural areas. The steep cliffs are also a popular nesting site for rare stormy petrels and shags, as well as puffins and also a species of cormorant only found on the Balearic Islands. Ibiza and Formentera are very popular with botanists and zoologists because much of their flora and fauna has not been fully researched.

People and customs

Ibiza and Formentera have a combined population of 80,000, with around 5,000 living on Formentera. Forty-five percent of the islands' people come from mainland Spain (mainly Andalusia) or from abroad (particularly Great Britain). In the summer, the number of foreign

Farmers at Sant Francesç

visitors rises sharply – mainly due to tourism which attracts many seasonal workers from all over Europe.

As rural life on Ibiza and Formentera had always been an isolated one, ancient traditions dating back to the Phoenician, Roman and Moorish eras survived until the 1960s. Then tourism made its appearance. Part of the population gave up agriculture completely, or only continued with it during the winter or at weekends, while many farmers sold their houses and land in order to invest in the development of resorts along the coasts.

As a result, this process of modernisation suppressed the old customs, forcing them into a decorative corner. Farmers' wives dressed in the traditional dark folk costume are a rare sight on Ibiza these days. The old courtship ritual, for instance, is now nothing more than an idyllic memory: in the *porxu*, or main room of the farmhouse, young men would play cards and drink wine, while at the other end of the room a young woman in her Sunday best would be talking with a suitor. In the middle of the room, the girl's mother would crack almonds, weave garlic into bundles or sew. The card players would wait their turn to talk with the girl – the future bride. By throwing stones they would indicate to whoever was talking with the girl that he had exceeded his permitted time.

This courtship ritual was a fixed part of island life. If the suitor wanted to express particular admiration for the girl he would fire a shot into the ground in front of his beloved on Sunday while going to church or while dancing. If he felt unjustly treated and rejected he would fire the shot very symbolically at the ground behind her.

Another ancient tradition that existed long before the advent of the telephone and the motor car was *es missatge* – shouting messages from house to house. This was used most often when someone had died, to summon people for the funeral. The name of the deceased would be shouted

Reconquest Day in Eivissa

Festive costume

The big day

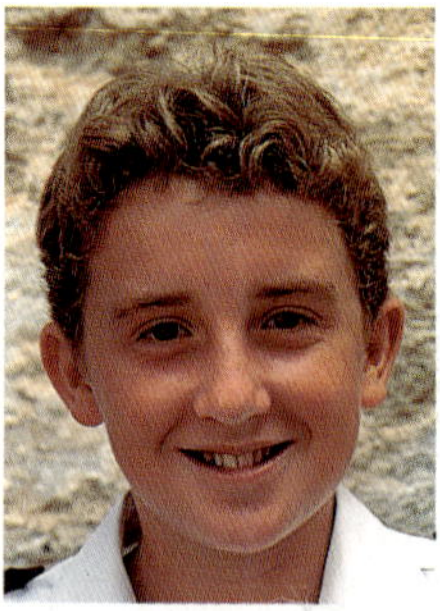

Facing the future head on

The summer crush

from house to house, along with '*¡En pau descansi!*' ('May he/she rest in peace!'), a phrase that was supposed to prevent the spirit from becoming a ghost, and is still heard today whenever the dead are mentioned. As soon as the news reached the last house, the occupant had to go to a nearby stone or tree and communicate the message to it, or someone in his own family would die before the year was out.

Tourism has altered many of the old customs, and reduced some to folklore and kitsch, but has also given people new roles: the Ibiza women who were formerly housewives and only travelled to town once a year have now become self-confident, emancipated individuals who are very often better educated than their husbands. The young men of today start working at a very early age, usually in the resorts, while the girls use the time before marriage to work towards professional qualifications. It's not unusual, therefore, for women to work at the reception desks of international hotels or as schoolteachers while their husbands work as barmen or waiters.

Language

Today's younger generation is fighting for a self-confident identity of its own, and language has become an integral part of this. Unusually it represents less of a reaction against foreigners than what is seen as Catalan domination of the local culture. 'We speak *Eivissenc*, not *Català*' is a phrase often heard on Ibiza, and the islanders only half-heartedly support the reintroduction of Catalan as the official language, especially in schools and administration. Indeed, nowadays, with their strong business sense, many islanders are far more eager to have their children learn English and German.

Economy

The economy, once based on agriculture, fishing, handicraft and salt panning, has undergone enormous structural changes as a result of the boom in tourism. In 1965, subsistence farming accounted for 45 percent of the workforce; today the figure is less than 10 percent. Today's salt panning is largely done by machines, and fishing has now become more of a hobby than a means of existence. Handicraft, construction and industry account for less than 20 percent of the islands' total economic strength, and the most successful of those is the fashion industry. The largest and most important sector of the economy is the service industry (hotels, restaurants, bars, shops, exchange outlets, etc.), which provides 58 percent of revenue by catering to the one and a half million or so visitors each year.

Tourism has been showing its dark side now, however: the behaviour of some young, predominantly British, visitors, mostly in Sant Antoni, has in recent years caused a certain amount of ill-feeling among locals and others, who find their drunken antics almost too much to bear. On the other hand, there are those who actively encourage it: bars with 'tequila slamming' sections, pushy bar staff, and pub crawls organised by holiday reps. As a result the island has gained a reputation off-putting to those in search of a peaceful family holiday, added to which are the obvious environmental problems such as lack of water, refuse disposal and nature conservation.

Island themes

Politics and administration

Together with Mallorca and Menorca, Ibiza and Formentera make up the autonomous region of the Balearic Islands (*Comunidad Autonoma de les Illes Balears*), governed by the regional parliament in Palma de Mallorca. Members of parliament for Ibiza and Formentera have 13 of the 59 seats. Like all autonomous administrations of Spain, the *Govern Balear* has far-reaching powers extending to agriculture, fisheries, trade, industry, tourism, health, transport, culture, education, sport, public buildings and including a partial say in Spain's economic and financial policies. Some of these powers are the responsibility of an island council, known in the *Pitiuses* as the *Consell Insular d'Eivissa i Formentera*.

Ibiza is divided into five parishes: Eivissa, Santa Eulària, Sant Joan, Sant Antoni and Sant Josep, all controlled by the conservative PP (*Partido Popular*). This party is finding it difficult to limit the amount of construction activity on the island, especially in Sant Josep, the largest and richest parish. The people of Ibiza don't like to be given orders by Madrid, Palma, or even their own island council; and Formentera does its best to avoid being influenced by Ibiza. In fact, both islands would most prefer to be independent realms of their own.

Consell Insular

The night is yet young

Historical Highlights

Ca 2000BC The megalithic dolmen grave of Ca Na Costa on Formentera is built. It is the only evidence today of population by the prehistoric Pitiusa people.

700BC The Carthaginians build a settlement at Sa Caleta in the southwest of Ibiza.

654BC The Carthaginians found Ibosim (Eivissa), which gradually starts to prosper, partly as a result of salt trading.

5th century BC The interior of the island gradually gets inhabited. An underground necropolis 50,000 sq m (59,500 sq yds) in size is built at Puig des Molins.

2nd century BC After the destruction of Carthage in the Third Punic War, Ibosim falls into Roman hands as a federal city, managing to retain a degree of independence: the name is Latinised to *Ebusus*.

70BC Under the Emperor Vespasian, Ebusus becomes *Municipium Flavium Ebusitanum*, an important Roman municipality in the province of Tarraconensis (Tarragona). It has the right to mint its own coins, and trade in salt and lead becomes increasingly important.

AD380 Christianity becomes established on Ibiza as the Roman state religion.

426 Ibiza and Formentera become part of the Kingdom of the Vandals which lasts for almost 100 years.

535 After the victory of the Byzantine general Belisar over the Vandals, Ibiza and Formentera become a part of Byzantium.

711 The Moors defeat the last Germanic rulers in Spain and also occupy the Balearic Islands. Islam is established as a second religion alongside Christianity, but the political situation remains unstable.

902 The Caliph of Córdova conquers Ibiza and the Balearics, renaming the island *Medina Iabissa*; highly sophisticated systems of irrigation and terracing are introduced.

1014 The empire of Córdova disintegrates and Ibiza and Formentera, along with the other Balearic Islands, become part of the Muslim *taifa* (small kingdom) of Denia on the Valencian mainland in Spain.

1114 A Catalan-Pisan penal expedition is sent to fight pirates taking refuge in the Balearic Islands, which fails on Ibiza.

1235 The Catalans conquer the Balearic Islands in the name of the crown of Aragón and repopulate them after the Moors have been driven out. The five sections of Ibiza, Alhaueth, Xarch, Benizamid, Portumany and Algarb are renamed Pla de Vila, Quarto des Rei, Balanzat, Portmany and Ses Salines. New administrative order accompanies the return of Christianity.

1276 Ibiza and Formentera become part of the newly founded Kingdom of Mallorca, remaining under Mallorcan rule until 1343.

1299 Jaume II of Mallorca institutes the *Universitat*, an autonomous organ of the Balearic Islands, which administers Ibiza and Formentera until 1717.

1343–1937 A long period of historical oblivion. Political events on the mainland have little effect on the islands.

1469 The marriage of Isabella of Castile and Ferdinand of Aragón paves the way for a Spanish national state.

16th century Numerous attacks by pirates reduce the rural population of Ibiza, which gradually grows impoverished. Formentera has already been abandoned.

1554 During the reign of Charles V (as Spanish King Carlos I) construction work begins on a new city wall at Eivissa, according to plans by Italian architect Giovanni Battista Calvi. The wall takes 30 years to complete and is paid for with the proceeds from the sales of salt from the salt flats (*salinas*).

1652 In Dalt Vila (the Upper Town of Eivissa) 520 people are killed by the plague.

1674 A chronic shortage of grain affects the western Mediterranean causing famine on the Balearic Islands.

1697 Repopulation of Formentera begins.

1715 The Castilians win the Spanish War of Succession and occupy the *Pitiuses*, which had fought on the side of the Habsburgs.

1717 Felipe V replaces the *Universitat* with a Castilian island administration, and the islands' salt becomes the property of the Spanish crown as punishment for supporting the Habsburgs. Ibiza and Formentera both grow more and more impoverished.

1782 Pope Pius VI authorises the establishment of an Episcopal See in Eivissa, which receives its civic charter from King Carlos III.

1867 The Habsburg archduke Ludwig Salvator, widely considered the Balearic Islands' first ever tourist, visits Ibiza.

1907 Charred gold medallions and terracotta figures are unearthed in a cave (Es Cuiram) near Cala de Sant Vicenç.

1908 Spain signs the agreement to end piracy, already negotiated in 1856. It marks the end of piracy and buccaneering on Ibiza.

1933 The first hotels are built on the islands.

1936–39 The Spanish Civil War. Ibiza and Mallorca are strongly nationalist. Fighting on Ibiza lasts from 8 August to 20 September 1936, after which Franco's Falangist troops take control of the island.

1958 The airport on Ibiza is opened, marking the start of mass tourism. Cheap, ugly developments start to appear.

Late 1960s Hippies settle on Ibiza in search of an alternative lifestyle.

1975 King Juan Carlos I becomes head of state and steers Spain to democracy.

1983 Under Spain's new democratic constitution, the Balearic Islands are accorded the status of an autonomous region.

1986 Spain joins the European Community.

1991 Approval of the LEN (Ley de Espacios Naturales), designed to protect the natural reserves of Ibiza and Formentera.

1992 Spain hosts the Olympic Games helping Ibiza attract the rich and famous to its shores.

1995 The salt pans on Ibiza and Formentera are finally declared nature reserves.

1998 Ashamed at the behaviour of some British visitors in Sant Antoni, the British consul, Michael Birkett, resigns his post.

How the Catalans conquered Ibiza

'Thou shalt not covet thy neighbour's wife!', runs one of the Ten Commandments. In the year 1235 it was the Emir of Iabissa's failure to observe this that resulted in his downfall.

During the Moorish period, which lasted from 711, Eivissa was given three walls that separated it into three different sections. The Dalt Vila contained the mosque and the emir's palace. With its 30 watchtowers the town seemed impregnable, all the more so in that the different parts of it were able to defend themselves independently. The Count of Barcelona had already failed to capture it during his punitive expedition of 1114, but in 1235 the Catalans, led by the Archbishop of Tarragona, were luckier: as part of the *reconquista* of Moorish territory, Archbishop Guillem de Montgrí received permission from Jaume I of Aragón to conquer Ibiza. On 8 August 1235 his troops finally invaded Eivissa after a siege of uncertain duration.

The conquerors made mention of an extraordinarily brief battle: 'They took the town ... after the *trabuco* (catapult) had thrown just two rocks.' This quick success is explained by a legend that has been passed down through generations: apparently the Emir had been dazzled by the beauty of a female slave from his brother's harem, and had abducted her. As a result, his brother was so furious that he opened a secret door and allowed the besieging army access to the city through a tunnel.

Today that historic August day is celebrated with a procession to the Chapel of Sant Ciriac, located on the presumed site of the secret tunnel. That same afternoon all of Ibiza meets up on Es Soto hill, beyond the town wall, for a watermelon battle in honour of the events of 1235.

Eivissa from the sea

Preceding pages: Torre d'es Savinar and the island of Es Vedrà

The Promenade

Armour Court in the Upper Town

Route 1

Eivissa

An Old Lady with a New Look

Eivissa (pop. 28,330), the 'white city' also known as Ibiza Town, shows its most attractive side to those approaching it slowly by ship. Entering the harbour, one can appreciate why artists and writers have been so captivated by Ibiza. The New Zealander Janet Frame (born 1924, *An Angel at my Table*), for instance, described the island as an 'is-land, a land of simple and beautiful being'.

The gently undulating landscape behind the capital has often been compared to a sleeping beauty. Dominating the city is the original Gothic cathedral, with several magnificent houses beneath it owned by influential families. The old centre is surrounded by a massive defensive town wall and, below, the dazzlingly white houses of the former fishing quarter gradually fall away to the sea.

In the early morning, a veil of mist lies over the town; as the day progresses, the light becomes harsher, as does the noise from the more modern part that is steadily expanding northwards. In the shady alleyways of the Dalt Vila, or Upper Town, however, the ambience is relaxed all day, and it is here that the island's history can be felt most.

History

Eivissa was founded by the Carthaginians in 654BC as *Ybsm*, or *Ibosim* (Carthaginian script has no vowels), and soon developed into a prosperous trading centre and important naval base. Ibosim was minting its own coins as early as the 5th century BC. In the 2nd century BC, after the Third Punic War and the destruction of Carthage, the island fell to the Romans, who valued it highly not only for its delicious figs, its delicate *garum* (a paste made from fish innards) and its well-made amphorae, but also for its currency which at that time was in great demand right across the Mediterranean.

Until 70BC *Ebusus*, as the Romans called it, enjoyed the privileges of an independent city. Under the Emperor Vespasian, however, it was forced to become Roman and lose its independence, remaining *Municipium Flavium Ebusitanum* for the next 500 years. From AD424 to the arrival of the Moors in 902, the town's history is rather unclear. It is known that the Vandals visited the island, but did not settle it, and in around 535 the Byzantines drove the Vandals out of the Mediterranean and took at least formal possession of Ibiza and Formentera as well.

During the Moorish epoch the town was known as *Medina Iabissa*, and numerous agricultural innovations gave the island a new lease of life. The Arabs also erected three defensive walls around the town, which successfully withstood numerous attacks by Christian crusaders. It was only in 1235 that the Catalans finally took the town and drove the Moors out for good. The conquerors decided to keep the sophisticated irrigation system and the terraces the Moors had left behind, and also accorded the city several generous privileges (freedom from taxes and military service and the freedom to trade). In 1299, the relatively democratic and autonomous *Universitat* was established, and it remained the centre of administration for the island for the following four centuries. It was only in 1715 that Ibiza's independence finally ended after the War of the Spanish Succession.

The impressive defensive wall dividing up the old town dates right back to Moorish times. It separates the historic site into three sections: *L'Arraval* (Lower Town), *Vila Mitjana* (Middle Town) and *Dalt Vila* (Upper Town), and was also very useful to the Catalans. During the 16th century, the development of new weapons and firearms necessitated a new and more resistant structure. This was commissioned in 1554 by the Holy Roman Emperor Charles V (King Carlos I) and the work was begun but not completed by the Italian architect Giovanni Battista Calvi. His successor Jacobo Paleazo Fratín extended the project to include the hill of Santa Llucia in the fortifications, and it was in this region that the *Vila Nova* (New Town) came into being.

Apart from the *Vila Nova*, the four clearly distinguishable parts of Eivissa known collectively today as Dalt Vila still contain numerous sections of the medieval fortifications, and the original course of the old town wall can clearly be seen from the 30 watchtowers (several of which are now nothing more than ruins.

The Romans left their mark, here at Portal de ses Taules

Entrance to the Upper Town

Sleepy by day, wide awake at night

Down by the harbour

The harbour area of La Marina and the fishing quarter of Sa Penya *See map below*

If you arrive in Eivissa by ship the **Monument al Corsaris ❶**, the obelisk commemorating the corsairs from Ibiza, located right in front of the harbour building, is one of the first sights you see. The corsairs, probably considered mere pirates by their victims, had a letter of manumission from the Spanish king which allowed them to raid and plunder ships in the Mediterranean from the 17th to the 19th centuries – but of course they also pro-

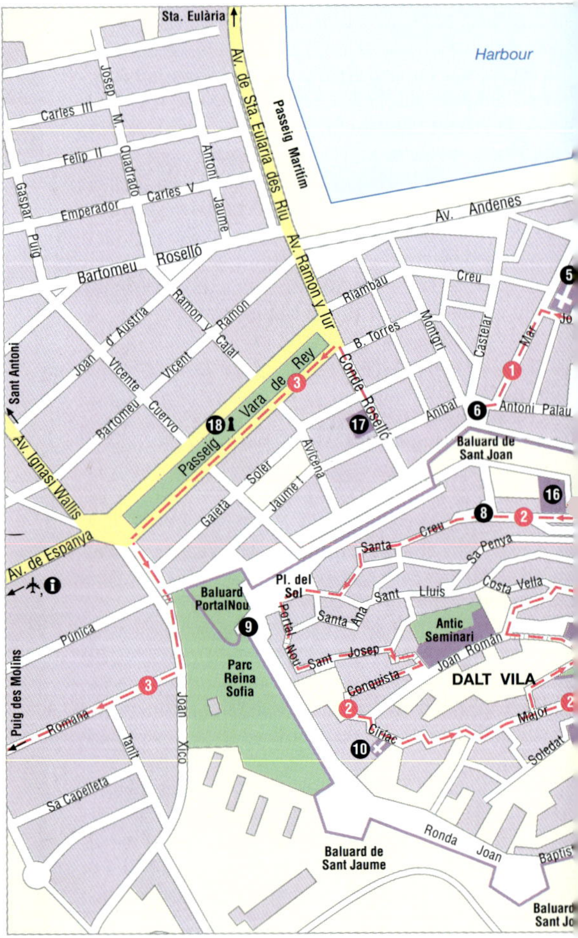

Corsar Monument

tected the island from attacks by enemy pirates. The monument was built in 1906 to mark the 100th anniversary of the day the English schooner *Felicity* was seized off Eivissa by the heroic Antoni Riquer – an event watched with great enthusiasm from the town wall by the people of the city.

Follow the Passeig des Moll in the direction of the harbour mole, past the former fishermen's houses with all their ground-floor bars, and you will see a small tower at the very end, which was, in fact, rebuilt in 1994. This is the **Sa Torre** ❷, the only fortification for the harbour quarter of ★ **La Marina** and the fishing quarter of ★ **Sa Penya** above it. The view of the town wall which runs right along the top of the cliff here, with the church of Sant Domènec behind, is definitely worth photographing.

Sa Torre and the Formentera ferry

Sa Penya views

Carrer de la Verge

The narrow street named ★★ **Carrer de la Verge** (also Carrer de sa Mare de Deu) runs from Sa Torre through the former fishing quarter. On warm summer nights it is the busiest street in town, full of bars and restaurants and boutiques selling *Moda Ad-Lib* clothing, a free and easy mix and match style evolved from the hippies. Here and in the Carrer d'Enmig, situated slightly lower down and accessible via a series of narrow flights of stone steps, you'll certainly find the right kind of slightly crazy outfit that Ibiza is famous for.

This main street looks very different on 16 July each year, when it fills up with long processions of people singing and praying. On their shoulders they carry the statue of the *Virgen del Carmen*, patron saint of fishermen and mariners, from the church of Sant Elm to the harbour, and place it inside a flower-bedecked boat. Then it leads a colourful procession of boats across the harbour.

Life is especially busy and hectic at two places in particular: the fish market of **Sa Peixateria** ❸, right beneath the city wall, and the food market of **Es Mercat Vell** ❹ on the Plaça de la Constitucion. The fish market is housed inside an octagonal structure and is surrounded by a jumble of small shops and old bars, and the food market is in a bright, pillared hall just a short walk away. Both institutions were opened in 1873 and have been an integral part of life on Ibiza ever since, providing a meeting place for housewives, old-age pensioners and tourists alike.

Christ the Redeemer

Just a stone's throw away from the food market is the ★ **Església Sant Elm** ❺, which has housed the famous *Virgen del Carmen* statue since 1702. The statue was originally kept in the Capella del Salvador not far from the cathedral, and many attempts were made to rename the church after the statue. Note that the statue of Christ inside the church is not the usual figure suffering on a cross with a crown of thorns, but instead looks astonishingly healthy, with short hair and a welcoming gesture: Christ the Redeemer (*el Salvador*). Sant Elm has been destroyed and rebuilt several times over the centuries; the last occasion was during the Spanish Civil War. The church once offered refuge from pirate attacks, because the defensive tower at the southeastern end of the harbour and the S'Estacada fortification at the northwestern end of this part of the city was not adequate.

Plaça de Sa Font

Follow along the Carrer del Mar now, or (a short cut) follow the original course of the fortifications along the Carrer Guillem Montgrí, until you reach a small square with a fountain, the **Plaça de Sa Font** ❻. The fountain dates from the 18th century and was quite a novelty in its day, as groundwater from the surrounding area was collected and provided the town with a proper water supply for the very first time. Until then each household had collected rainwater in private cisterns – a custom which still exists out in rural areas.

City Route 2

Bringing the past back to life in the Dalt Vila

From the harbour, enter the ★★★ **Dalt Vila** by passing through the **Portal de ses Taules** ❼, which is flanked by two headless Roman statues: the left one is of a Roman legionary or general, and the right one of the goddess Juno. The drawbridge is a copy of the original one, which was replaced for quite some time by a stone bridge. The gate leads into the former guards' courtyard, where the pillared portico was used for the first hippy market of the 1970s.

During medieval times, the adjoining **Plaça de la Vila** ❽ – now framed picturesquely by boutiques, restaurants, craft shops and art galleries – was an esplanade in front of the old fortress where festivals were celebrated. The gate to that old complex was located at the western end of the square, where the Carrer de la Santa Creu begins. The two gate towers still survive: one is an art gallery and the other is part of a residential building.

The ★ **Carrer de la Santa Creu** lies right at the centre of the L'Arraval quarter. With narrow streets and huddled houses, it acts as a kind of 'extended living room' for the local inhabitants on warm summer evenings. The rooms inside the buildings are small and tend to trap the heat, which is why they prefer to sit in the cooler evening breeze outside. Wide-open doors let in the cool air, television sets blare away, and the strangers walking past are scrutinised, providing an endless topic of conversation

Portal de ses Taules

Reconquest Day procession

Easter penitents

with the neighbours. The Dalt Vila is a quiet place with no exciting nightlife, as there are no discotheques here. The Plaça del Sol does provide a fine view of the city after dark, however, and is a popular meeting place.

The Portal Nou

The worn stone steps of the **Portal Nou** ❾ (New Gate), next to a tunnel at the eastern side of the Plaça del Sol, lead away from the old town; this route was used in the old days by farmers on the way to their fields. Defenders also used to pour boiling oil and pitch over the heads of invaders from a horizontal embrasure just above the gate.

The picturesque flight of steps on the left side of the tunnel leads into the Carrer Sant Josep, flanked on the right by the remains of the old Moorish wall which used to separate the lower from the middle town. Two of the old watchtowers can still be made out.

At the end of the Carrer Sant Josep on the left is the little 15th-century **Església del Hospitalet**, which served as a workshop for the famous GAT theatre group until the beginning of 1996. Another flight of steps leads visitors into the street where the clash of Catalan sabres brought the Moorish epoch to an end in 1235 – hence its name, the Carrer de la Conquesta.

Capella de Sant Ciriac

The Catalans probably gained access to the Moorish citadel through a secret tunnel, the entrance of which is thought to be located behind the tiny **Capella de Sant Ciriac** ❿ (built in 1754 and recently renovated) in the street of the same name.

A few steps further on, the Carrer de Sant Ciriac connects with the Carrer Major, or Main Street, which leads into the centre of the Dalt Vila. Houses with familial coats of arms above their entrance arches, well-tended inner courtyards, broad staircases and high Gothic windows all testify here to the wealth and prosperity of the former inhabitants. Sickness and disease were also rife, however, as the various alleyway names make clear: Carrer de la Soledat, Carrer de l'Hospital and Carrer de l'Esperanca. The Carrer de la Soledat is not often used: it runs along the edge of the old cemetery and is rather like some enchanted garden path, with all its arbours overgrown with bright pink bougainvillea.

The inhabitants of Dalt Vila and La Marina were rivals for centuries. The Upper Town, hidden behind its thick wall, was inhabited by governors, landowners, officials, clerics and officers, while the mercantile *petit bourgeois* population down by the harbour (craftsmen, tradesmen and seamen) referred to their counterparts up there as *mossóns* (peasants). The other got their revenge by calling the people from the Lower Town *banyaculs* ('bum-bathers', a reference to the proximity of the sea).

The Upper Town took things too far at times, however: once, when a pirate raid threatened, they simply had all

Promenade at the top of Dalt Vila

the houses in the Lower Town demolished, so that the pirates would have no walls to hide behind. That left the inhabitants of La Marina hopelessly exposed to any attack from the sea. It was only when the danger of pirate raids finally receded for good towards the end of the 18th century that they could finally breathe more easily and put the arrogant and feudal *mossóns* in their place.

At the summit of Dalt Vila is the ★★ **Plaça de la Catedral**, the traditional secular and spiritual power centre of the city and the island. Enter the square from the Carrer Major and you will see the late Gothic structure that once housed the royal courts of law, or *Reial Curia*. There is a good view of the harbour and much of the island from the observation point just beside it.

Traditional costume on Plaça de la Catedral

The lengthy building on the left-hand side of the square once had three establishments under its one roof: **La Universitat** in Mudéjar style (a Spanish-Islamic style that developed after the Christian *reconquista* in the Middle Ages); then the Gothic **Capella del Salvador** (Chapel of the Redeemer) with its pointed arches; and to the right another, smaller chapel in the baroque style. The entire structure today houses the ★★★ **Museu Arqueològic** ⓫ (May to September, Tuesday to Saturday 10am–2pm and 5–8pm; October to March 10am–1pm and 4–6pm; Sunday 10am–2pm, closed Monday and holidays).

A portcullis between the cathedral and La Universitat blocks the way to a staircase leading into the casemate of the bastion, Baluard de Santa Tecla. This vaulted room, once a storage chamber, is also part of the archaeological museum, which was founded in 1906, and excavation finds have been exhibited here ever since; enter it from the Plaça de la Catedral. The grave goods from the Punic necropolis on the Puig des Molins *(see page 27)* are on display inside a newer building on the Via Romana.

The ★★ **cathedral**, built between the 14th and 16th centuries on the foundations of a mosque and a Roman temple, and consecrated to *Santa Maria de las Nieves* (St Mary of the Snows), is distinctive for the pragmatic simplicity of its Catalan Gothic style: more inviting than soaring, with very little Mediterranean light penetrating the interior through the tiny windows. Baroque additions inside have spoilt many of the clear Gothic lines, though the apse still survives. A small museum above the sacristy contains several fine altar panels (14th to 18th centuries) and liturgical instruments.

Virgin and Child in the Cathedral

Beside the cathedral to the west, and separated from it by the small Carrer de l'Universitat, is the fortress, **Es Castell**, which is now being renovated bit by bit after years of neglect. The work is taking a long time because the body financing it, the Consell Insular, still cannot agree on its future use. This, combined with poor building work, has led to several structural problems: the new staircase on Sa Torreta watchtower, for instance, has been defaced by machine-cut sandstone, and the old Phoenician foundation walls have been covered over. When the old stairs were pulled down, a cistern dating from that time was discovered; now the only clue to its existence is an aperture in the wall beside the steps.

Since the castle is still closed to visitors, the best view of it can be had from the ★ **Baluard de Sant Bernat** ⓬. In good weather you can see all the way to Formentera from this stunning observation point, and the different parts of the old castle can clearly be made out too: on the left, a watchtower from the old Moorish fortress, and beside it the former royal governor's residence with its unusual sloping roof.

Moorish remains uncovered

Beneath the next tower there is a tunnel leading down to the rocky overhang **Es Calvari**, which slopes southeastwards down to the sea. Then come the Torre del Homenaje ('Tower of Homage') and the prominent reddish-coloured **Almudaina**, or castle, at the highest point of the city. The street that descends from the Almudaina, the Ronda de Joan Baptista, is now open again after lengthy renovations and excavations. Remains of the old Moorish wall, with its entryways and old watchtowers, can be made out. There is a school of thought saying that the entrance to the secret tunnel used by the Catalan invaders may have been located here.

Returning to the Carrer Major now: the ★ **Portella d'en Serra**, once a gate in the old Moorish fortifications, provides access from the Carrer Major to the Carrer de Santa Maria. The two towers that once defended this gate still survive: on the right, Sa Torre des Canonge, and on the left (and now part of a house), the Can Balansat. The Carrer de Santa Maria had two names from the 15th century onwards: the inhabitants of the Dalt Vila called it the *camí d'anar a la mar* (the way to the sea), while the people of the harbour quarter called it the *camí d'anar a missa* (the way to the church). Now with just the one name, the Carrer de Santa Maria leads behind the **El Corsario** ⓭ hotel and restaurant and into the Plaça d'Espanya.

El Corsario has quite a history: it was built as a pirates' palazzo in the 17th century. The small hotel, which has a great view from its restaurant terrace, enjoyed its greatest popularity in the 1950s. That was when the island's artists used to congregate for endless discussions, and Group '59 (*see page 61*) held its first exhibitions in the rooms here. El Corsario was also reputedly the place where Clifford Irving first had the idea of forging the autobiography of eccentric millionaire Howard Hughes, a subject later treated by Orson Welles in his film *Fake*, which was shot on Ibiza.

Instead of staying on the Carrer de Santa Maria you can also take a detour to the Plaça d'Espanya by turning left next to El Corsario and going up the Carrer del Pintor Mariano Tur de Montis, which ends in a broad flight of stone steps. There you will reach the **Antic Seminaria**, a long building that housed a Jesuit priests' seminary from 1669. The Societas Jesu only stayed here until 1767, however, the year the order was driven out by the anticlerical and enlightened Spanish king Carlos III. The building adjoins a watchtower that once guarded the Porta de J. Francolina, a gate that controlled access in medieval times to the Vila Mitjana with its many parks and gardens. From here a hairpin bend leads into the Carrer Pere Tur, the 18th and 19th-century houses of which already belong to the Vila Nova.

The Town Hall courtyard

The Plaça d'Espanya is dominated by the ★ **Ajuntament** ⓮ or Town Hall. After secularisation in 1838, the Town Hall was established in the former Dominican monastery, where monks had been living since 1558. Their refectory became the hall of sessions for the town council.

Numerous outdoor concerts and theatre performances take place in the inner courtyard of the Town Hall. Classical concerts are also held in the former monastery church of **Sant Domènec** (17th-century) with its striking domed roof and baroque interior. The view from the terrace in this square extends as far as Formentera.

Church of Sant Domènec

The Baluard de Santa Llucia to the northeast once enclosed the hill of Santa Llucia. The largest of the defensive bastions in Eivissa (there are seven altogether), **Es Polvorí** ⓯, was once used for storing gunpowder. The original structure was destroyed in a massive explosion after it was

Dalt Vila from the Baluard de Sant Joan

struck by lightning in 1730, and the bang (*es tro*) is still mentioned in a colloquial expression on the island: *Es més vell que s'any d'es tro* ('That must have been before the year of the thunderclap'), which is used to describe anything extremely ancient or antiquated. There is an excellent view from the Baluard de Santa Llucia of the Sa Penya quarter.

On the Plaça de sa Carossa, between the bastions of Santa Llucia and Sant Joan, a bronze memorial commemorates the local historian, poet and archivist Isidor Macabich (1883–1973). The city's greatest son sits in the shade of large eucalyptus trees, a life-sized figure with an open book on his knee. There are many tales told of Macabich, whose major claim to fame was a four-volume *History of Ibiza*. Once, when asked if his family was the noblest in the city, Macabich replied: 'My son, there are no nobles in Eivissa. We are all fishermen, farmers or bastards.'

Museu d'Art Contemporani

The next bastion on the route, the Baluard de Sant Joan, once contained an armoury and an underground magazine. Two floors here are taken up by the **Museu d'Art Contemporani** ⓰ (Museum of Contemporary Art; Monday to Friday 10am–1.30pm and 5–8pm, Saturday 10am–1.30pm; closed Sunday), where exhibitions change every three months and *tout Ibiza* shows up for the occasion. Collections have recently included unknown works by the German avant-garde artist Joseph Beuys.

An access tunnel for road traffic was broken through the Baluard de Sant Joan in the early 1970s, and provides an interesting 'cutaway' view of the interior of this mighty structure. From the top there is an impressive view of the old part of Eivissa, and you can follow the course of the old city wall if you simply let your gaze wander from watchtower to watchtower – starting at the cathedral.

City Route 3

Outside the city

Teatro Pereira – Passeig Vara de Rey – Puig des Molins

It was in 1898 that the **Teatro Pereira** ⓱ was the first building to be erected outside the city walls. Eivissa had finally broken free of its centuries-old medieval constraints – the three rings of fortifications, the bastions and the S'Estacada harbour wall – and could develop and expand. A business area quickly grew up around the plush new theatre, which began by showing variety performances and not allowing women inside. Now the foyer has an art deco-style jazz bar, where cool drinks accompany cool music.

Today, the ★★ **Passeig Vara de Rey** is the heart of everyday life in Eivissa. People come here to see and be seen, and brief flirts sometimes get prolonged over a coffee outside the **Montesol**, the oldest hotel on the island. This ancient establishment has all the decadent grandeur of a colonial hotel, and its cafeteria contains a cross-section of all those who consider themselves special: yuppies from the nearby banks and offices, blue-blooded island nobles, wealthy hippies with credit cards, and so forth.

In the middle of the promenade square, the **Monument a Vara de Rey** ⓲ commemorates the popular general Joaquin Vara de Rey i Rubió, who died in the Cuban war in 1898, during which the Spanish lost their last American colony. The monument, officially opened in an avenue of poplars in the middle of open countryside in 1904, soon received a fitting backdrop: all the houses in the square today were built between 1913 and 1935 in neo-colonial style. The area is now a pedestrian precinct, and several pleasant bars have recently appeared.

Monument a Vara de Rey and colonial houses in the square

If you follow the road along the city wall, ascend the stairway to the left and turn right halfway up, you will reach the historically significant Via Romana. This is where the most important archaeological site on the island, ★★★ **Puig des Molins** (Mill Hill) is located, surrounded by olive-trees. This hill was famed only for its windmills until 1903, when a Phoenician necropolis was discovered beneath it containing 4,000 tombs and an enormous amount of grave goods. The catacomb-riddled hill is the most important Phoenician site in the Western Mediterranean. It served as a necropolis from 650 to 200BC. Since the Carthaginians regarded Ibiza as sacred ground, many of those who could afford to do so had themselves brought to the island to be buried. Roman oil-lamps indicate that their successors continued with the custom for some time.

Puig des Molins: catacombs

The **Museu Monogràfic del Puig des Molins** (May to September, Tuesday to Saturday 5–8pm, Sunday 10am–2pm; closed Monday) at the foot of the hill documents the rich finds from the necropolis, and also includes exhibits from other ancient sites on the island. The evidence points to the existence of a high culture of great sophistication: sarcophagi and grave goods, household items, coins and jewellery.

City Route 4

Eivissa's nightlife and the Botafoc Lighthouse

Far de Botafoc

The Casino

Until the late 1960s, the region where all Eivissa's discotheques and night clubs are now located used to be part of the park and garden area known as Ses Feixes. The allotments northeast of the old town and west of the Passeig Maritim provided fruit and vegetables for the townspeople. The gardens were not fenced in, but marked by typical gates with slanted posts topped by an oblong beam; a few of these still survive. Of Moorish origin, the gardens were irrigated by a skilfully devised network of drainage channels. There are plans to redevelop the thicket-covered area behind the **Pacha**, the island's oldest discotheque.

Quite a few visitors to Ibiza have to wind down when they get home, because the nights here are long: it's around midday when the last guests are ushered out of the all-night discos. Anyone eager to discover the notorious nightlife of this island should head for the harbour in Eivissa, sit on the Passeig de Moll and stare at the passers-by from one of the bar terraces, keeping an eye out for one of the sharply dressed *relaciones publicas* distributing invitations to the discos. Anyone dressed crazily enough gets free admission.

The ★★ **Passeig Maritim** on the northwestern edge of the harbour basin was built in the 1980s at around the same time as the **casino**, near the Pacha disco, which established the area as an entertainment district.

From the marina, there's a short walk and some delightful views across the sea and the city to the ★ **Far de Botafoc** (Botafoc Lighthouse), which has stood for centuries on the Illa Grossa and shown ships the way into the safe harbour. On the way you pass **Platja des Duros** (Coin Beach), which connects the Illa Plana peninsula (used as a quarantine station during plague outbreaks) with the lighthouse island. A swimming contest to the lighthouse is held here at the beginning of August each year as part of the Fiesta de Nuestra Senyora de las Nieves – and everyone is allowed to take part!

Ses Salines beach

Route 2

Hotel skylines and bird sanctuaries

Eivissa – Ses Figueretes – Sant Jordi de Ses Salines – Ses Salines (12km/7 miles) *See map on page 31*

This short route into the southwestern part of Ibiza has several surprises in store. With its hotel skyline, the town of Ses Figueretes, largely swallowed up by Eivissa, forms a transition to the busy beach Platja d'en Bossa. It's difficult to imagine that this region was once the wealthiest on the island, earning its money from windmills, agriculture and salt pans. This change becomes particularly evident in Sant Jordi de Ses Salines, but just beyond it, in the village of Sant Francesç de S'Estany, the old Ibizan atmosphere returns. Today the once-important salt pans are a delightful nature conservation area and important bird sanctuary.

This tour can easily be done by bicycle, but also by bus or even on foot, and takes from three hours to one day depending on your choice.

Bar sign in Ses Figuertes

Ses Figueretes was a purely agricultural region until the late 1950s, but since then, with the advent of tourism, has grown into a booming suburb of Eivissa. The nearest beach to Eivissa, it is lined with hotel towers, holiday apartments, restaurants and bars. The next strip of coast is the **Platja d'en Bossa**, which already forms part of the municipality of Sant Josep. This is the longest tourist beach on the island – and beach life is most definitely celebrated. Anyone keen on watersports has come to the right place: visit the **Centro de Buceo Anfibios** for sailing or diving, and the **Escuela de Windsurfing** or the **Club de Surf Ibiza** for surfing.

Sant Jordi's Space Disco

Església de Sant Jordi

Sant Francesç de S'Estany

A little further inland, **Sant Jordi de Ses Salines** was caught up in the construction boom of the 1970s, and all that remains of this formerly modest village is the ★ **Església de Sant Jordi**, which has provided salt pan workers with religious succour since the Middle Ages. Like most churches on Ibiza it has fortifications: thick walls, battlements and embrasures. The side chapels were built in the 18th century, after the danger of pirate attack had receded.

Beyond Sant Jordi, in the direction of Sa Canal, the landscape is largely unspoilt. The tiny village of **Sant Francesç de S'Estany**, seems quite untouched by mass tourism. Its small church is the only one on the island without a cemetery – apparently because the high salt content of the ground here would more or less preserve the dead.

Until 1996 the little church was a place of pilgrimage for Andalusian migrants celebrating the *rocio* to honour the Madonna of the Dew (*Virgen del Rocio*). Owing to conservation problems this happy pilgrimage has been transfered to the Hipódromo de Sant Jordi, an old racing course. Any southern Spaniard who cannot celebrate the *rocio* in his home village (quite likely at the beginning of the tourist season) takes part. At 6pm on the first Saturday in May, flower-bedecked coaches and jeeps set off from Eivissa, accompanied by singing and clapping pilgrims in colourful Andalusian traditional dress. They spend the night beside campfires, dancing and singing. The next morning a short prayer is said to the *Virgen del Rocio*.

A good detour from here is to a tower next to the sea known as the **Torre de Sal Rossa** (or Torre des Carregador), one of the oldest watchtowers that used to encircle the entire island. If the danger of pirate attack was imminent, the workers loading ships at the salt pans were warned from the tower by smoke signals.

The salt pans of ★★★ **Ses Salines** extend across the plain behind Sant Francesc as far as the **Puig des Falco** (Falcon Hill), and symbolise the independence, sense of community and democratic self-administration of the Ibizans. They were used by Carthaginians, Romans and Moors, before being made public property by the Catalonians in the 13th century. Even though the pans are owned by a private company today, all Ibizans still consider them as theirs; this feeling of public property resurfaced in 1977 when a long campaign to keep Ses Salines a conservation area began. The area has always been a paradise for migrating birds: herons, storks and even flamingos stop here during the winter on their way to North Africa. It was finally declared a nature reserve in 1995.

On the right-hand side of the road, the chain of hills known as **Es Corb Marí** (Cormorant) rises to elevations

Ses Salines salt pans

Es Cavallet beach

A ready supply of salt

Platja de Ses Salines

of 160m (525ft). It was here in 1936, after the invasion by Franco's troops, that numerous inhabitants of Eivissa who were considered *rojos* ('reds') sought refuge; among them were the poet Rafael Alberti and his wife. The thick forest and caves made the hills a very good hiding-place. Many of the hills and towns in the area are named after birds, and a great many nest here: fish eagles and cranes can even be spotted in the winter, next to ponds.

Another detour you can take is to ★★ **Es Cavallet**, one of the two official nudist beaches on Ibiza. Shortly before the road ends at Sa Canal, a smaller route branches off to the left in the direction of the sandy beach of Es Cavallet, around 1.5km/1 mile away. Families keep to the top end of the beach, while further along is a predominantly gay section. On the way there you pass a mountain of sea salt on the right, where many Ibizans come to shovel up their supply of salt for the year. The narrow road then winds its way through salt pans and past an old paddle-wheel as far as the sea, where there are several fine views of Dalt Vila in the distance and also of the magnificent sand-dune landscape. If you like Caribbean dance music, the restaurant here by the beach is the place to go.

Soon **Sa Canal** and **Platja de Migjorn** (known collectively as Platja de Ses Salines by the locals) come into view. The sheer number of cars in the huge car park makes it clear that this is the most popular and fashionable beach on the island. In August the place is only ever deserted in the very early morning, when the 'beautiful people' are either still dancing in the discos or finally in bed. They meet up again at 3pm for their first cocktail outside the **Malibu** or go and lie in the dunes. The 'in' place to be is around the bars at the centre of this vast beach, while families prefer to settle down at the northwestern and southeastern ends. There's usually a quiet spot to be found at the very end of the beach, just where the rocky point known as Punta de Ses Portes begins.

The watchtower **Torre de ses Portes** on the southernmost peninsula of Ibiza probably dates from the 16th century. In 1750 it was given three cannon so that the strait between Ibiza and Formentera's island of S'Espalmador could be kept safe.

The small salt harbour of **Sa Canal** at the other (northwestern) end of the Platja de Migjorn is certainly worth a visit. It was here, long before tourism arrived on Ibiza, that the locals learnt their first broken English from the predominantly Scandinavian sailors on the salt ships. They were referred to as *jans*, a term possibly deriving from the Catalan word *gegants* (giants), because of their immense stature.

Picturesque Cala Vedella

Route 3

The beautiful southwest

Eivissa – Sa Caleta – Sant Josep de Sa Talaia – Cala d'Hort – Sant Agustí d'Es Vedrà (53km/32 miles including detours) *See map on page 31*

This route into the southwest of Ibiza features a dramatic and idyllic mixture of colours and landscapes. Picturesque beaches in small coves alternate with strips of farmland, and the legendary rocky island of Es Vedrà, just offshore, can be seen almost the whole time. There are very few concrete high-rises along this route, but quite a few holiday settlements (ancient as well as modern). It's best to go by car in order to take in all the detours, but if you prefer to cycle there are places to spend the night in Sant Josep, Cala Vedella and Sant Agusti.

The small bay known as ★ **Sa Caleta** is 11km (6 miles) away from Eivissa, on a flat section of rocky coast that culminates in the long stony beach of Es Codolar. Sa Caleta is a very popular beach with local families, and many own traditional boathouses. During Sunday swims and picnics hardly anyone realises that it was once here, on the plateau out on the peninsula, that the first Phoenicians settled on the island over 2,500 years ago.

Boathouses at Sa Caleta

Phoenician settlement

The foundation walls of this settlement were only exposed a few years ago. Several buildings of various sizes, small streets and squares, and also a community oven for baking bread all point to the former importance of this site. The Phoenicians must have considered this location quite ideal, with its fertile hinterland, sea view and offshore island. They soon discovered an even better site, however, when just 50 years later they abandoned Sa Caleta and founded Ibosim, today's Eivissa. Some politicians are still keen to turn Sa Caleta into a trading harbour once again, but are encountering fierce resistance from the population.

Hidden away just behind this peninsula is a small bay that is very popular with the locals. They refer to it as **El Rincón del Marino** (Mariner's Corner), even though its real name is Bol Nou. This is nothing unusual as many places have two or more names on Ibiza, and they are often spelt in a number of ways. Today this corner is especially popular with courting couples as it is sheltered on three sides from view as well as from the wind by high walls of sandstone.

Cala Jondal

A good detour at this point (2km/1 mile) leads to **Cala Jondal**, a partly stony and partly sand-filled bay. It can be reached via a track (turn left off the Sa Caleta road in the direction of Cova Santa), which follows the winding course of a dried-up stream. Exotic-looking villas with plenty of domes and pillars can be seen up on the slopes, with views across the beach and towards Formentera. Beach bars and restaurants attract a very mixed public here. On warm summer nights the bars offer live music and art exhibitions as alternatives to the disco scene.

Just before the road to Sant Josep there is a signpost on the left to **Cova Santa** (April to October daily, 9.30am to 1.30pm), a limestone cavern that was discovered in the 15th century and was frequently used as a hiding place during raids by Moorish pirates. It is called the 'Holy Cave' because, according to legend, a hermit once gave its waters healing powers.

The town of ★ **Sant Josep de Sa Talaia** (pop. 10,000) lies at the foot of the highest point on Ibiza, the mountain known slightly confusingly as Sa Talaia de Sant Josep

Beach bar at Cala Jondal

(475m/1,550ft). The town is the capital of the largest and most prosperous municipality on the island, which extends eastwards as far as Eivissa and north as far as the bay of Sant Antoni, thus covering the most important tourist area of Ibiza. Sant Josep itself, once just a small village with a church, a bar and a few shops, has definitely grown over the past 20 years: it now has supermarkets, bars, restaurants, a post office, banks, medical services and much more. There are also several art galleries.

One sight worth seeing is the **Església de Sant Josep**, which was consecrated on St John's Night in 1731. Since the pirate raids had virtually stopped during the 18th century, this church is less fortress-like than most others on the island. It contains several important works of art, including an altar painting dedicated to St Joseph by the Mallorcan painter Pere Bosch, dating from 1735; the original painting was destroyed in a fire during the Spanish Civil War, however, so today's work is merely a reproduction (1958). The craft shops and art galleries here sell all kinds of different craft products such as hand embroidery, ceramics, filigree gold and silver jewellery, musical instruments, and also paintings by local artists like Bobermann and Jussara.

Take a detour (6km/4 miles) at this stage up to the top of ★★ **Sa Talaia de Sant Josep**, which can be reached via a rain-washed track. Behind the radio tower marking the highest point on Ibiza there is a picnic area with wooden tables and benches, and a superb panoramic view of the entire island.

From Sant Josep a delightful stretch of winding road leads southwards towards the sea, providing repeated glimpses of remote white farmhouses on hilltops, and elegant terraces up on the slopes. Another good detour here leads to ★ **Es Cubells**, a village very untypical of Ibiza because of its location right next to the sea and also at the foot of a steep section of coastline. The village lies on the site of a hermitage where the Carmelite monk and mystic Francisco Palau once lived. Today Es Cubells has a school, a church, a supermarket, a bar – and a restaurant with a spectacular view of Formentera.

The highlight of this round trip is without a doubt the breathtakingly beautiful stretch of coastline before Cala d'Hort, with the island of ★★★ **Es Vedrà** (Sleeping Dragon) offshore. The Catalan author Josep Pla (1897–1981) wrote, 'Es Vedrà is one of those wonderful things one never ever forgets.' It rises steeply from the sea to a height of 381m (1,250ft), and when viewed together with its smaller sister island of **Es Vedranell** from the Es Savinar tower viewpoint, it really does resemble a dragon's back. Pla also admired the colour of Es Vedrà, 'A whitish

Església de Sant Josep – pulpit

Souvenirs in Sant Josep

The coast at Es Cubells

Es Vedrà from Torre d'es Sanivar

Atlantis – a haven for hippies

colour that seems to be shot through with the greenish and bluish tones of glass.'

The weird and wonderful atmosphere of Es Vedrà is confirmed by the wealth of legends surrounding it. According to one of them, Vedrà was the island of the Sirens in Homer's *Odyssey*. It has also been accorded a kind of magnetic energy: many boats that have dared approach it closely despite the danger of underwater reefs have reported malfunctions or complete breakdowns in their navigational instruments. In 1855, the monk Francisco Palau felt irresistibly attracted by Es Vedrà. He left his cell at the hermitage in Es Cubells, and sat in a cave on the island to meditate – and on his second day there he had a vision of light which spoke to him. Several other sensitive people have had visions here; one of them insisted that the light he saw came from underwater aliens…

Es Vedrà is a very popular nesting-place for falcons and seagulls. There were numerous goats living on it until 1950, when the last of them was killed by hunters; the Consell Insular finally decided to reintroduce the animals to the island in 1994.

Other sights along this part of the coast include the watchtower of Es Savinar, and Ses Paisses de Cala d'Hort, a Phoenician country estate dating from the 5th century BC – and they all add to the mythological magic of this region. The massive round tower known as the ★★ **Torre d'es Savinar** stands on a rocky outcrop, and provides a fine view of the 'Sleeping Dragon' below. On the left you can see the ochre-coloured sandstone cliffs of Sa Padrera bay, which ends at Cap Llentrisca in the southeast. Large blocks of stone were once quarried from this bay to build the city walls around Eivissa.

During the 1970s, hippies renamed this region Atlantis because of its peculiar 'vibrations'. Known to the locals as *peluts* ('the hairy ones'), the hippies used to spend entire summers living in the cave here that was once used by pirates, and produced several cave paintings, including one of a Buddha.

Es Vedrà can be appreciated in its full majesty from the gravel beach at ★ **Cala d'Hort**, with its numerous seafood restaurants. The colossal island resembles some massive stone cathedral, its colour changing constantly depending on the time of day. The less romantically inclined can also find windsurfing, pedal-boat and waterskiing facilities here, though reaching the sea does involve a slightly uncomfortable walk across the rocks.

One good detour leads along a bumpy and dusty track to **Cala Carbó**, a small sandy beach in a narrow lagoon, where two excellent seafood restaurants more than reward the effort to get here. Another equally worthwhile detour is to the ancient Phoenician estate of ★★ **Ses Paisses de Cala d'Hort**. Along the road to Cala Vedella, a right turn leads towards Sant Josep. Around 1km (½ mile) further on is a sign pointing to a Phoenician-Roman site. This ancient estate is a fine example of how the different powers that conquered Ibiza often made the best of their predecessors' achievements rather than simply destroying them. First built by the Phoenicians in the 5th century BC, the estate was extended by the Romans in the 2nd century AD as a villa. The Byzantines then occupied it until the 8th century. The whole site was first discovered in 1917, and excavated between 1982 and 1985. The foundation walls of a large house can be seen, along with several outbuildings for agricultural purposes such as mills (for oil and grain), and also two necropolises. The Phoenician one contains 20 tombs carved out of the rock-face, and two vaults dating from the Byzantine period are located at the upper part of the site.

Cala Vedella is a small and picturesquely situated bay, and naturally has lots of holiday apartments, bars, restaurants, boutiques and tiny discotheques as well. In wintertime the whole place is deserted, when it actually has a certain strange charm.

The route now continues past several comfortable-looking holiday villages, and three well-patronised beaches which seem to blend into each other: Caló d'en Real, Cala Molí and Cala Tarida.

After Cala Tarida, travel 6km (3 miles) inland to the picturesque village of ★ **Sant Agustí d'es Vedrà**, which tourism has luckily passed by until now. A small church, a little bar, a restaurant, and a local store that sells tobacco and serves drinks make a refreshing and simple change from the over abundance of facilities elsewhere.

Sant Agustí d'es Vedrà (above) and outlook from Cala d'Hort

On the road from Santa Agnès to Sant Antoni

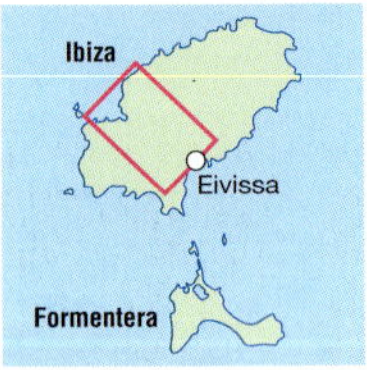

Route 4

The Ibizans' favourite excursion

Eivissa – Sant Rafel de Sa Creu – Santa Agnès de Corona – Sant Antoni de Portmany (42km/26 miles)
See map on page 31

For centuries life on Ibiza was played out on the soil of the islanders' own self-sufficient farms. However, since now the average family owns two cars, the locals like to spend their weekends exploring their island. The route they usually take begins at Sant Rafel, which still has a delightful rural atmosphere despite its proximity to Eivissa, and the world-famous KU discotheque (now called Privilège). The road from there to Santa Agnès leads through some truly pastoral landscape. After a very attractive stretch of road beside the sea on the other side of Sant Agnès, the route lands up unexpectedly in the busiest tourist resort on the island: Sant Antoni de Portmany, located in the largest bay on Ibiza. Because of the various detours, not all the places on this route can be reached by the public bus network; cyclists can spend the night in Sant Antoni.

The coast near Santa Agnès de Corona

Sant Rafel ceramics

A short while ago, the town of ★★ **Sant Rafel de Sa Creu** was nothing more than just another inland village on the road between Eivissa and Sant Antoni. Tourists only knew the name because of the nearby **Privilège** and **Amnesia** discotheques. The new bypass has now given the town an opportunity to retain its village atmosphere, and this is combined with an excellent selection of inexpensive restaurants serving local as well as French, Argentinean and Tex-Mex cuisine; make sure you book well in advance, however, because all the tables tend to get taken, especially at weekends. The Consell Insular has declared Sant Rafel a *zona de interés artesanal* because of its three ceramic workshops, where the potters can be observed at work. There is also a delightful little church (1785).

After the stopover in Sant Rafel, continue along the road towards Santa Agnès, passing cornfields filled with fig trees. You'll see the odd *noria* now and then – hand-operated wells with waterwheels up to 30m (98ft) deep and 5m (16ft) wide. A short break halfway for a picnic or a *torrada* (barbecue) can be enjoyed in the ★★ **Torrent de Buscastell**, one of the island's finest river valleys, now dry. The orchards and orange groves in this region are still watered using largely traditional methods, and the trusty spring called Es Broll at the top of the valley fills the canals of an ancient irrigation system. There were two serious forest fires here in Buscastell in 1975 and 1987, and even though traces from it can still be seen in a few places it is astonishing how quickly the landscape has regenerated.

Regenerated forest in Buscastell

Halfway to Santa Agnès there are some strange-looking holes in the ground surrounded by rocks at the side of the road. These are ovens that were once used to burn limestone, in order to make the whitewash for house walls. At the highest point of this stretch, where the forest stops and the view opens on to a broad valley, it's easy to understand why the local inhabitants also call the village there ★★★ **Santa Agnès de Corona** (Crown of St Agnes). In January the valley is a fantastic sight from here, covered with thousands of blossoming almond trees.

The small, simple village church near two restaurants and a shoe and leather shop on the edge of this fertile valley make up the heart of Santa Agnès de Corona. The school, other shops and the residential part are all dotted along the valley and up the slopes.

The private ethnological museum **Can Pujol** is located near the shop Cas Farré, which unlike the official one in Santa Eulària (*see page 51*) provides a true depiction of traditional life on Ibiza, can unfortunately only be visited during the festival of St Agnes (21 January). The bare, scrubbed rock shows through the floor of the storage room, revealing how it has been integrated into the entire building, and the upper parts of the kitchen walls are blackened by soot rising from the hearth. The only thing that jars is the bar inside the *porxu* (living room/entrance hall).

Old kiln near Santa Agnès

Santa Agnès: artisan at work

Two routes branch away from the village square: the one to the right ends up at **Sant Mateu d'Aubarca** (*see pages 44–5*) and the other to the left leads down to the sea. If you don't mind an unsurfaced stretch of road you will be rewarded by one of the most exciting views of the steep coastline from Sant Mateu, and there are also plenty of good hiking possibilities: the bizarre rock chimneys of **Es Castellar** over to the right, with the almost inaccessible bay of **Ses Balandres** below them and views to the island of **Ses Margalides** with its rock arches; and over to the left, the rocky promontory of **Cap Negret**.

Ses Fontanelles coast near Cova des Vi

Sa Capella restaurant

Go back to Santa Agnès now and continue with the route. Behind the shop Cas Ferré, the road towards Sant Antoni leading into the mountains crosses a very unspoilt-looking section of landscape, with several beautiful views out to sea (and as far away as the 80-km/49-mile distant mainland on clear winter days).

From the settlement at Can Germà there's a good detour (1.5km/1 mile) to the beach of **Cala Salada** with its fine sand. From there it's about half an hour on foot northwards to the **Cova des Vi** cavern on the strip of coast known as Ses Fontanelles. Prehistoric cave paintings were discovered here several years ago, but can scarcely be made out today; protective iron bars have been placed over them. It's the thought that counts, however, on this atmospheric walk.

Shortly before Sant Antoni there is a small church hidden away from the road on the left, which has now been converted into the Sa Capella restaurant. The Basque food it serves has been appreciated by several famous people including Sting, Tom Hanks and Bruce Springsteen. The purple sign saying ★★ **Sa Capella de Santa Agnès** does not refer to the restaurant, however, but to a subterranean chapel beneath it (Monday 9am–noon, Saturday 7–9pm) named after a wooden statue that appeared in the cave in the 17th century. Discovered in 1907, the underground chapel contained several cult objects from the Phoenician, Roman and Moorish periods, all pointing to its use as a pagan cult site. It consists of a small rectangular nave and a choir section with a simple altar.

The town of ★★★ **Sant Antoni de Portmany** (pop. 10,400) is the administrative capital of the region of the same name, which extends from Sant Mateu in the north to Sant Rafel in the south. As recently as 1965, this town on the northern flank of Ibiza's largest bay consisted of just a church with a few houses and hotels, but since then it has grown to become a tourist resort with a skyline and nightlife to rival the Benidorms, Arenals and Palma Novas of this world.

Contemporary sculpture in Sant Antoni

The bay with its much-vaunted sunrises and sunsets attracts predominantly young tourists of all nationalities. The innumerable bars and discos in the 'west end' make the summer twice as hot, and Ibiza's young people meet here the whole year round too to spend their weekends at techno parties on the **Ruta del Bacalao**. The raves begin on Fridays at sunset in the **Café del Mar** and end at sunrise on Sundays in the **Play 2** disco or the **Es Paradis.** The latter establishment is famous for driving out its guests almost ceremonially by hosing them down with large amounts of water.

After such long nights hardly anyone is awake enough to attend mass in the ★ **Església de Sant Antoni**, which stands at a very dignified location: it has been proven that a chapel and a cemetery stood on the same site in 1305. The church's present appearance goes back to the 17th century, and because of the dangers of pirate raids it was built as a defensive structure. The church is entered via a large front courtyard, with the presbytery and an entrance hall (*porxu*) to the left of it. The choir is the oldest part of the structure. Along the nave are nine chapels, dedicated to various different saints, and there are some notable paintings here such as *The Ecstasy of St Anthony* and *Holy Physicians*. At the back of the building there is an attractive little square, where the bare stone of the church wall is exposed.

Daytime pursuits, West End

The promenade at Sant Antoni runs directly beside the sea, affording an unobstructed view across the broad bay that forms a natural harbour. The Catalans derived the name Portmany from the Roman name *portus magnus* (great harbour) and that is what they continue to call the town locally. Original names for places are heard far more often on Ibiza than the saints' names, e.g. an Ibizan will happily refer to Santa Agnès de Corona as *Corona*, pure and simple.

The **Passeig de Ses Fonts** has two fountains which are illuminated at night on public holidays. This promenade is as full during the day as is the 'west end' at night, brimming with people waiting for the excursion trips or simply strolling, having their portraits painted or being caricatured, eating ice cream in the many cafés, enjoying English breakfasts, and so forth. At the end of the harbour mole you may be lucky enough to see the fishermen returning to port and passing on their catch to the various restaurants.

There are numerous beaches, coves and small bays in the immediate vicinity of Sant Antoni, many of them easily reached by bus or by boat. One particularly nice beach with turquoise water is the ★★ **Cala Comte**, where several small niches provide protection from the wind or unwelcome looks, and there is also a unique view of the islands of S'Espartar, Illa des Bosc and Ses Bledes. The sunsets here are still romantic, unlike those in the crowded, built-up bay of Sant Antoni, and a nighttime walk up to the 18th-century Torre de Comte watchtower can also be very atmospheric.

Cala Comte

Route 5

The quiet side of Ibiza

Eivissa – Sant Miquel de Balansat – Port de Benirrás – Sant Mateu d'Aubarca – Santa Gertrudis de Fruitera (60km/40 miles, including detours)

Harvest time at Sant Miquel de Balansat

The further you drive north from Eivissa, the quieter the whole island becomes. In summer as in winter, Santa Gertrudis is a meeting point and information centre for all islanders of non-Spanish extraction, and not just because of the town's central location geographically. Next on the route is the town of Sant Miquel de Balansat, situated on a hilltop and pleasantly quiet despite its tourist amenities. After sampling a few of the delights along the northwest coast of the island, the route ends at the still unspoilt wine village of Sant Mateu d'Aubarca from where there are wonderful views and where you can abandon the car and go for a walk. This day trip is best done by car; the main towns have twice-daily bus connections with Eivissa.

If we pass by Santa Gertrudis on the way there, the first proper stop on this route is ★★ **Sant Miquel de Balansat.** It lies at the end of an almost perfectly straight section of road with various rural restaurants and orchards along it. Sant Miquel de Balansat is situated on a high plain at the northern end of a chain of hills, and has steadily expanded over the past 25 years. Its organically developed infrastructure and numerous service industries have given the prosperous little town far more freedom from Eivissa's influence than most other inland towns: supermarkets, restaurants, bars, cafés and boutiques guarantee every modern amenity imaginable.

Old Sant Miquel can still be experienced on the hilltop around the church, from where there is a fine panoramic view of the surrounding land. Invitingly shady plane trees and low houses give everything a pleasant village atmosphere, and the idyll isn't even spoilt by the boutique and souvenir shop here. Small marble-topped tables out in the street point to the presence of a bar, and relaxed old men can often be seen playing dominoes or chess at them. The oldest bar in the village also functions as a tobacconist and a post office.

The ★★★ **Església de Sant Miquel** (16th-century) is thought to be the oldest church on the island if a document dated 1784 (a letter from the local priest to his bishop) is to be believed. This fortified church has a magnificent nave with Gothic arches, and together with its side chapels forms a ground-plan in the shape of a cross. The Capella de Benirrás, built in 1691, has very graceful paintings on its walls and ceiling, restored by an international team of specialists in 1994; the entrance arch of the chapel is known locally as the *Porta de ses Dones* (Women's Arch).

Folk dancing takes place in the churchyard every Thursday from 6pm, and the priest explains everything to the numerous guests in six different languages. Miguel Pallarés, organizer of the dancing, won the popular Ramón Llull prize in 1998. On the same day, artisans from the surrounding area display their handmade wares for sale in the grounds of the S'Hort centre (a renovated farmhouse below the church).

The road winds its way further north now through the valley of a dried-up stream, and then down to the natural harbour of ★ **Port de Sant Miquel de Balansat.** Two high-rise hotels on the right-hand side of the harbour blend in well with the steep hillside, and restaurants, bars, souvenir shops and even a small discotheque complete the tourist infrastructure of this pleasant holiday resort.

At the northwestern end of the bay, a small path leads around the hill and into the sheltered bay of **Cala des Moltó**. There is a good view from here of the small island

Església de Sant Miquel

Port de Sant Miquel de Balansat

of Illa Murada, and the watchtower **Torre d'es Molar** is just a short walk away.

From Port de Sant Miquel a road leads northeastwards behind the hotels to the limestone caverns known as the ★★ **Coves de Can Marca** (daily 10am–1.30pm and 3–7pm, admission fee). Over 100,000 years old, these caves were discovered by smugglers and used to hide contraband. Red and black signs still mark the route to the second exit. Grotesque limestone formations, stalagmites and stalactites create a bizarre subterranean world, where cave explorers recently discovered the bones and fossils of long-extinct animals (primarily birds).

Coves de Can Marca

From Can Marca you can follow the route for another 4km (2 miles) as far as the beach at ★ **Port de Benirrás**, or alternatively travel there along the well-surfaced road from Sant Miquel. The gravel beach at Benirrás has been provided with sand. This 'tropicalisation' procedure (common on many Mediterranean beaches) has come in for a lot of criticism from environmentalists, because the sand continually gets washed back into the sea and stifles the flora and fauna on the sandbanks offshore.

With a large bay surrounded by steep mountains, Benirrás is a perfect natural harbour, and is teeming with sailing boats throughout the summer. Inspired by the protected site and its romantic backdrop, the hippies began a 'full moon festival' tradition that continues to this day and has lost none of its gay abandon.

A worthwhile detour on the way from Sant Miquel to Sant Mateu d'Aubarca leads to **Portitxol**, where the view from the top of the steep coast is fantastic, despite the half-built holiday village. Keen hikers will appreciate the challenging descent to the sea, plus the climb back up.

Boating fun and full moon festival at Port de Benirrás

It's definitely the most unspoilt village on the whole island: ★ **Sant Mateu d'Aubarca.** The building regulations here are very strict, and the beach is not easily accessible, so touristic development has been ruled out for the future, especially since the entire stretch of coast between Portitxol and Cap Nonó is a nature reserve. The village has thus found another means of making money: it makes wine. The surrounding valley has been turned into one enormous vineyard, where grapes Ibizan and foreign ripen slowly in the sunshine. A wine festival is held each year at the beginning of December, and there is even a brand of Ibizan *cava* (sparkling wine) to sample while enjoying the dancing, singing and poetry readings.

The 18th-century **Església de San Mateu** derives much of its charm from its black-and-white tiled floor, and the nave is lined on both sides by nine side chapels. These, together with the broad *porxu* (entrance hall), give the church its relaxed appearance.

All routes towards the sea are ideal for lengthy strolls or hikes. One good excursion is to the **Cala d'Albarca** and the **Punta de Ses Torres** (roughly 9km/5 miles there and back if you visit both), where a strange structure of natural stone still baffles experts as to its original function.

Sant Mateu shows its colours

The landscape between Sant Mateu and Santa Gertrudis de Fruitera is typically Ibizan and unspoilt, with numerous examples of the local rural architecture. The town of ★★★ **Santa Gertrudis de Fruitera** has developed into a fashionable and very popular village in recent years. Three bars and three restaurants now cater for the steady stream of visitors, who come here even in wintertime.

The **Bar Costa**, also known as the Bocadillo bar, has a great reputation for good (and inexpensive) food. Almost every inch of the walls in the bar is covered with paintings by local artists, but these constitute only a small part of what is probably the largest and most comprehensive private collection of local art anywhere on the island. The bar owner accepted paintings as payment in kind for food and drink from impoverished artists, and his generosity has paid off because several of his former patrons have become very famous, with their pictures changing hands for very high sums. One such artist is Vicent Calbet, who died in Japan in 1994. This bar and those nearby are almost always filled with artists both genuine and aspiring.

A few doors further on the Casi Todo junk shop sells all kinds of fascinating articles, and the **Can Daifa** – architecturally the most interesting house in the village – sells art and antiques. This unique cultural atmosphere has now attracted an international bookshop, which also has its own small art gallery.

Santa Gertrudis de Fruitera, a cultural centre

Traditional transport near Sant Lorenç de Balàfia

Route 6

Typical Ibiza – harmony in contrast

Eivissa – Sant Llorenç de Balàfia – Sant Joan de Labritja – Sant Vicenç de sa Cala – Es Cuiram (83km/51 miles with detours) *See map on page 42*

This route into the northeast of the island has several contrasting elements. It starts with an Arab fortress that was later used as a base by Moorish pirates, before passing through mountainous countryside and round hair-raising hairpins, and then several busy holiday villages. Sant Joan de Labritja is a fascinating mixture of traditional and modern, and the tiny village of Sant Vicenç de sa Cala, perched high up on the other side of the Serra de Sant Vicenç massif, is rather like arriving at the end of the world. This illusion quickly shatters, however, when the resort of Cala de San Vicenç comes into view. Nevertheless, in this bay are the remains of the Phoenician cult site of Es Cuiram.

The town of **Sant Llorenç de Balàfia** lies 8km (5 miles) inland from the coast as the crow flies, but has still been a popular target for pirate raids down the centuries. The reason was probably the fertile plain of **Es Pla d'Atzaró**. The farmers took refuge from the pirates inside the hamlet of ★★ **Balàfia**, with its three fortified, doorless towers. They entered using rope ladders, which they then pulled in, waiting until the lookout gave the all-clear. The name and age of this picturesque group of buildings have led many to assume they were built during the Arab epoch, which was why the Moorish pirates knew about them.

Balàfia looks very much the way many traditional Ibizan houses used to: they were not painted white orig-

Going to market

inally for reasons of camouflage. The details were as attractive as they were functional: the herringbone pattern of the stones on the tower to increase the wall's resilience; the white crosses to ward off evil spirits; the natural stone paving both outside and inside the buildings; and the gates, made from *sabinas* (Phoenician juniper).

Apart from the fortified hamlet, the idyllic landscape and the ★ **Església de Sant Llorenç**, built towards the end of the 18th century by local architects Joan Mari d'Antoni Moreno and Joan Serra d'Antoni Armat, Sant Llorenç has little to offer the visitor. Many are hoping that things will remain so, and that the place will not lose its character.

The changes wrought to the original landscape are nowhere more evident than along the idyllic stretch of coastline between Xarraca and Portinatx. Here, on the western side of the northernmost point of the island, a remote tourist world unconnected with the hinterland and its traditions has grown up.

Welcome to Xarraca

In the ★★ **Cala Xarraca** itself, apart from a few slightly over-ornate private villas, the landscape is still largely as romantic and wild as ever. Just a few kilometres to the northeast, however, the tiny bay of **Portinatx** is packed with one holiday club after the other. One has even chosen the picturesque watchtower on the ★ **Punta de Sa Torre** as its backdrop. The Punta, a narrow promontory, has attractive beaches on both sides. Bars, restaurants and discotheques complete the tourist enclave.

Portinatx bay

To experience the impressive mountain landscape north of Sant Joan properly, take the unsurfaced and sometimes rather bumpy mountain road that leads southeastwards in the direction of Portinatx. Despite the recent new buildings, the pleasant town of ★ **Sant Joan de Labritja** still holds on to its very village-like atmosphere, which has attracted numerous artists and outcasts over the years. During the 1970s, when the search for alternative lifestyles reached its peak, the small village experienced a miniature population explosion; since then, the tobacconist and local store have been joined by several esoteric shops and establishments offering services such as faith healing astrology and tarot card readers. The local Ibizans seem to feel quite at home in these cosmopolitan surroundings, probably not least because the new arrivals seemed to confirm the benefits of their simple lifestyle. The 'in' place to meet is the **Bar Vista Alegre**, which serves all kinds of delicious food.

The ★ **Església de Sant Joan** was built in the 18th century, and unlike many other village churches on the island it has a tiled roof with barrel vault and a spire. The adjacent cemetery is typical of Ibiza: graveyards here take up relatively little space, because all the dead find their last resting place in one of the niches in the cemetery wall.

On All Saints' Day (1 November) every cemetery becomes a sea of flowers. Relatives tell each other stories about the deceased on the previous evening over a meal of *panellets* (special cakes with pine kernels) and pomegranates, and leave the half-empty table for the spirits of their dead loved ones.

Style-conscious youth

Beyond Sant Joan the road ascends steeply before descending in a series of hairpin bends to ★★ **Sant Vicenç de sa Cala**. Surrounded by the mountains of the Serra de Sant Vicenç, this village seems cut off from the rest of the island. The remote-looking church and the few houses dotted around seem to be from another world.

The houses are located very far apart in this area. A small shop with a bar and *estanco* (tobacconist) near the church, and another shop on one of the hills to the right of the main road provide the inhabitants with whatever they cannot produce themselves on their own farms. Not surprising, therefore, that the Consell Insular has just set up a *Camp d'Aprenatge* here so that students can learn a traditional way of life in its natural environment.

Cala de Sant Vicenç

After this encounter with solitude it comes as all the more of a shock to reach the **Cala de Sant Vicenç** at the other end of the valley where huge high-rise hotels line the broadest section of beach. The private holiday village on the Clot des Llamp to the north is especially eye-catching,looking out to the island of Tagomago.

Just a short distance to the north of the resort, below the forested Puig des Clapers (200m/650ft), is a Phoenician cult site in the cave of ★★★ **Es Cuiram**. In 1907, several terracotta figures were discovered here, all of the same female deity with similar characteristics (most commonly a high tiara). A bronze plaque with two inscriptions found 15 years later in the cave unveiled the mystery of the figures, which had been taken to the archaeological museum in Eivissa (*see page 28*). The first inscription, dating from the 6th or 5th century BC, is a dedication to the Phoenician gods Resef and Melkart, while the second refers to a sacrificial stone to the almighty goddess Tanit. Numerous partitions consisting of stalactites and stalagmites divide up the cult site into larger and smaller halls, where remains of animal sacrifices testify to a place of worship for the goddess Tanit from the 5th to the 2nd century BC.

It is possible to take a detour to ★ **Aigues Blanques**, a long and narrow nudist beach (one of the two official nudist beaches on Ibiza). Cars can be parked on a small rise the sea a 3-minute walk away. The sand is an attractive reddish-brown colour because of the nearby sandstone cliffs, and there are also two good beach restaurants.

Cap Martinet

Route 7

Eccentric and sophisticated – the east coast

Eivissa – Platja de Talamanca – Cala Llonga – Santa Eulària des Riu – Es Canar– Sant Carles de Peralta (62km/38 miles) *See map on page 42*

The land beyond the harbour of Eivissa, on Cap Martinet, is the most sought-after residential area on Ibiza for retired Britons and Germans, and the inevitable golf course is not far away in Roca Llisa. The largest and oldest hippy markets on this eastern part of the island add a touch of exoticism. The village of San Carles, once considered a hippy stronghold par excellence, is gradually adjusting to its sophisticated surroundings, and has hosted several high-quality classical concerts in recent years with top performers. Alongside the alternative lifestyles, this trip also provides several opportunities for a refreshing swim, whether in the sea or at the Aqualandia water park.

Talamanca

Talamanca extends from the northeastern part of Eivissa's harbour area to the **Platja de Talamanca** just beyond. Today it is a hotel and residential area. Formerly this region only contained the summer residences of the capital's wealthy. Beside it is the most expensive piece of real estate on the island, covering almost the whole of ★ **Cap Martinet.** The proximity of Eivissa and the picturesque view across the Dalt Vila explain the high property prices. There are also several fascinating experimental buildings here by the avant-garde architects Josep Lluis Sert, Erwin Broner and Gonzalo Rodriquez, which either develop or newly interpret several traditional features of Ibizan construction. This illustrious neighbourhood also contains **Aqualandia**, the largest water park on Ibiza. Visible for miles, it can be reached hourly by bus from Eivissa.

A good detour leads to the small, sandy bay of **S'Estanyol**, located behind the long hill on Cap Martinet. You can either take the scenic route around the cape, or the surfaced road from Talamanca (6km/4 miles there and back). This bay is favoured by people eager to escape the hustle and bustle of the busy beaches near the capital.

Detail of the altar painting in Jesús's church

From Eivissa, travel 4km (2½ miles) inland to **Jesús**. The ★★ **Església de Nostra Mare de Deu de Jesús** (Thursday 10am–noon) is the most important sight in this tiny village. Construction work began on it in the early 15th century and from 1549 it was used by Franciscan monks. In 1580 the Dominicans took over, and built a monastery in the nearby old town (Eivissa's Town Hall). The church contains the most important ★★ **altar painting** on the island, which comes from the Valencia studio of the brothers Juan Rodrigo and Francisco de Osona. It depicts scenes from the life of the Virgin and of the Apostles on seven panels. Painted in 1598, the work is a fascinating combination of late Gothic and Renaissance elements.

Cala Llonga

Beyond Jesús the road leads past the elegant residential area on Cap Furnet and the 253-m (830-ft) high Puig de Sa Creu to Ibiza's only golf course (*see page 69*) lying on a plateau of the Serra des Puig in the luxurious settlement of **Roca Llisa**. The slopes here are lined with numerous magnificent villas looking across to Formentera.

Another 3.5km (2 miles) further on is the bay of ★ **Cala Llonga**, nestling between the Puig de Ses Torrentes (220m/720ft) and the Punta Roja. The fine sand, shallow water and numerous sports facilities make Cala Llonga an ideal destination for any family holiday.

The route now leads past the long La Siesta residential area to the left, on the northwestern slope of the Puig d'en Pep (232m/760ft), and arrives immediately afterwards at ★★★ **Santa Eulària des Riu** (pop. 5,300), the third largest town on the island. The town is the administrative capital of the municipality of the same name, and although the Catalan conquerors renamed the place *Quartó del Rei* in 1235, the locals continued to call it by its Arab name of *Xarx* until well into the 14th century. The reason this area was populated relatively early on was because of its proximity to the estuary of the Riu de Santa Eulària, the only river on the island, which has its source in the mountains above Santa Gertrudis. The Arabs used the mouth of the river to irrigate numerous plantations.

Santa Eulària des Riu: the old bridge is for pedestrians only

Just outside Santa Eulària, two bridges connect the two banks of the *riu*, which only has water in very rainy years. The ancient stone bridge is for pedestrians only. But the most striking feature of Santa Eulària is the Puig de Missa

Tourist transport in the town

(52m/170ft), with the ★★ **Església es Puig de Missa** (visits by arrangement, tel: 330072) perched on top of it. The massive round tower on the other side of it points clearly to its original defensive character. It was built during the 16th century and, judging by its appearance, seems to have been the work of several different architects, who also designed the fortifications for Eivissa. As a fortress-church it not only guarded the sea but also the numerous water-driven mills beneath its walls, of which only ruins remain today.

The two side-chapels and the roofed-over courtyard were extended during the 17th century. The baroque high altar and the altar paintings in the side chapels were brought here from a church in Segovia in the 1950s, after the destruction of all the church's cultural artefacts during the Spanish Civil War.

Beyond the church, the town opens out in a fan shape towards the sea. The American, Elliot Paul, immortalised this view in his novel on the Civil War *Life and Death of a Spanish Town* (1937).

A relatively recent addition to Santa Eulària is the excellent ★★★ **Museu Etnològic d'Eivissa i Formentera** (Ethnological Museum; daily 11am–1pm and 5–8pm; closed Sunday and Monday morning) housed in the 300-year-old farmhouse of Can Ros. Traditional dress (*emprendada*), numerous domestic items, tools and weapons document farming life over the centuries; there's even a wine cellar to browse through.

On Wednesdays, if you like flea markets, it's worth planning a detour (roughly 5km/3 miles) via **Es Canar** on the way to Sant Carles. Even though the town itself doesn't have any sights worth seeing, the famous *mercadillo* (market) held in the grounds of the **Punta Arabi** holiday club

Punta Arabi hippy market

Maintaining traditions: olive press near Sant Carles and music making at the Las Dalias

has created a precedent for numerous other hippy-style flea markets all over the island.

In ★★ **Sant Carles de Peralta** the church and the bar opposite form the centre of social life. During the 'flower power' years of the late 1960s, when many people made a living producing craft goods, playing music or painting, the **Bar Anita** was the 'in' place to meet – not just because of the delicious *hierbas* (herbal liqueurs) that the owner Anita made according to ancient recipes, but also because of her friendly attitude towards her unconventional guests. During that very artistic era, one of the first hippy markets began in the garden of the **Las Dalias** restaurant outside San Carles, and its popularity soon brought numerous other artistic and cultural activities in its wake. Today Las Dalias is a kind of cultural centre with a gallery for art exhibitions and a small theatre, with a bar and a restaurant attached. Summer performances here have included items such as amateur plays by the English Theatre Trust and belly-dancing.

Sant Carles is not only a centre of hippy culture but also of classical piano playing. Since 1986 the local parish church has hosted an international piano competition, and the success of the event has now prompted the organisers to invite classical artists from all over the world at other times of year. As a result, San Carles is now *the* place to go to hear classical music, even though numerous other villages such as Sant Josep, Jesús and Sant Rafel, are doing their best to compete.

There are several beaches near Sant Carles which have the double attraction of beautiful landscape and delicious seafood. Nature lovers may consider Cala Nova, Cala Llenya and Platja des Figueral with their modern holiday villages as rather too built-up, but even so this part of the coast – with the east wind blowing across it, lively surf and bizarrely-shaped rocks – is definitely varied.

Cala Mastella, Cala Boix and Es Pou have retained much of their former beauty. The bay of **Es Pou d'es Lleò** was guarded by the Torre de Campanitx in former times, because it was often used by pirates during raids on Balàfia. If the simple little harbour restaurant with its delicious paella had existed at that time, they may well have spared the rest of the island.

Sign for the best seafood

The very best seafood restaurant on Ibiza is located at ★★ **Cala Mastella**, south of the promontory. Fish is brought here straight from the boat, and Don Bigote's wife cooks superb *sopa de peix* (fish soup) and grilled *lluc* (pike). The food is served at around 2pm on long, bare-topped wooden tables. If you want to make a reservation, though, you'll have to do it in person, as the host and his wife don't have a telephone.

Route 8

Formentera

Wind, sand and silence

La Savina – Ses Illetes – Es Pujols – Sant Ferran de ses Roques – Platja de Migjorn – El Pilar – Sant Francesc Xavier – Cap de Barbària (66km/41 miles with detours)
See map on page 55

Formentera is an island in the truest sense: a place of quiet forgetfulness where visitors soon lose all track of time and live in close contact with the elements of wind, sea and sand, all softened by the sun and the moon. From the moment the ferry docks at La Savina, the unhurried activity at the harbour makes it clear that this island has its very own pace of life. It's a world unto itself and is very easy to explore – especially by bicycle. The island bus also travels between La Savina and Mola twice daily.

Devote some time to this island and you will realise that small really is beautiful. The sights of Formentera can be seen in a day, but you need longer to experience the wind, sand, and silence.

Estany des Peix

History

Ibiza's sister island has undergone several phases of settlement and depopulation throughout its history. Archaeological evidence has proven that it was inhabited 4,000 years ago by a people who were socially well organised. When the Carthaginians founded a colony on Ibiza they included Formentera among their possessions without ever actually settling it. It was only after the Third Punic War, when Ibiza and Formentera became Roman, that they were

Rural idyll at Sant Ferran

probably used for growing corn by their conquerors. The name of the island could derive from the Latin word for corn, *frumentum*.

After the fall of Byzantium, Formentera only experienced an upturn in its fortunes when the Moors occupied it and Ibiza in 902, and introduced a system of irrigation. When the Moors were driven out by the Catalans in 1235, Formentera went through a period of decline because of numerous raids by North African and Turkish pirates. Famine caused by poor harvests and plague outbreaks almost killed off the entire population. The few survivors abandoned the island in the late 14th century and sought refuge on Ibiza.

For the next 300 years, Ibizans only visited Formentera to chop wood or pan salt. After the pirate attacks subsided during the late 17th century, the island gradually became repopulated. By the end of the 18th century, there were enough people on the island for the local bishop to divide it up into the three parishes of Sant Francesc Xavier, Sant Ferran de ses Roques and Nostra Senyora del Pilar.

La Savina waterfront

Bikes for hire

A trip across Formentera

The island harbour of **La Savina** (derived from the word *sabina* – Phoenician juniper) was only a mole made of natural stone a few years ago, where Formentera's simple exports – salt, wood and quarried stone – were loaded and shipped, or fishermen's nets dried in the sun. The harbour has now been extended and includes a marina.

When the passengers from the ferry have all disembarked and left for their various destinations, however, the whole place becomes very quiet again. All the travel operators' offices nearby have row upon row of bicycles outside them for hire.

The two seawater-fed lakes of **Estany des Peix** and **Estany Pudent** lie on either side of the road leading inland from La Savina. The name of the first lake makes it clear that it's good for fishing; all the locals have to do is close off the small channel leading to the sea. The name of the second means 'stinking pond', and refers to the days when it had no connection with the sea.

The road that runs northeastwards from the harbour between the sea and the Estany Pudent leads to the main destination for most daytrippers from Ibiza: the Platja de ses Illetes. On the way there, the salt pans of Ses Salines can be seen off to the right. They are closely connected with the pans on Ibiza. In 1985 they were closed down as economically unprofitable, and since then the whole area has become one vast nature reserve and the breeding grounds of many different kinds of waterfowl.

The nudist beach of ★★ **Ses Illetes** is an almost 3-km (1½-mile) long strip of sand on the narrow Es Trucadors promontory, which seems to extend all the way to the offshore island of **S'Espalmador**. Both are separated, however, by the 200-m (650-ft) wide channel called Es Pas, which you can wade across at low tide, if it is calm.

The bay of S'Espalmador, sheltered by the Illa de sa Torreta, becomes a forest of yacht-masts in the summertime. Strategically important until the 18th century, the island (3sq km/1 sq mile) has dunes, palm trees, a lighthouse, an old watchtower, and a *finca* (country estate).

On the eastern side of the spit is the ★ **Platja de Llevant**. They say the fine white sand of the dunes here is very good at providing people with quick suntans; whatever the case, this beach is still one of the most popular on Formentera.

S'Espalmador

To the south of the Platja de Llevant, beach after beach continues all the way to Es Pujols. Between the Platja des Canyers and the Platja des Pujols, a short distance inland (and not far from the Estany Pudent), is the megalithic tomb of ★★★ **Ca na Costa**. This complex, roughly 4,000 years old, consists of a circle of stone slabs up to 2m (7ft) high, and in 1974 the skeletal remains of six Stone Age people were discovered here. The men were aged

Formentera farmhouse

Sant Ferran and its church

between 40 and 45 when they died, and almost 2m (7ft) tall. One of the two women died between the ages of 30 and 35, the other between 20 and 25. Even though the bodies had degenerative bone diseases, they still had almost all their teeth. Earthenware pots and stone tools were found alongside them as grave goods. This stone circle, together with the second megalithic site of Cap de Barbària II (*see page 59*) and also various Bronze Age finds, prove that Formentera was settled as far back as prehistoric times – something its big sister Ibiza cannot claim (as yet).

The collection of hotels, restaurants, bars, discotheques and other places of entertainment that makes up ★ **Es Pujols** is only lively in the summertime. It's rather like a smaller version of Sant Antoni on Ibiza, and is primarily popular with young people. The watchtower on the **Punta Prima**, which marks the eastern end of the Platja des Pujols, was unable to prevent the invasion of these modern pirates; there again, rather than plunder and ransack they leave behind a small fortune, and are therefore well regarded.

Another place in which to stay up late and have a good time is ★ **Sant Ferran de ses Roques**. Those who would rather stay in with a good book should visit the **Biblioteca Internacional** in Sant Ferran, built up over 25 years by a Californian named Bob, who died in 1986. It contains an amazing 20,000 books. The ★★ **Església de Sant Ferran** is different from most others on Formentera and also Ibiza: it has no plaster or whitewash on its walls, and the terracotta colour of its brickwork contrasts sharply with the dazzling white of the nearby houses.

The narrow strip of land between the broad lowland of the island and the high plain of La Mola doesn't seem to provide much of interest at first, apart from long beaches on either side – but there are two sights hidden away here. The first is the limestone cavern of ★★ **Cova d'en Xeroni** (daily 8am–8pm) on the right-hand side of the road beyond Sant Ferran, which is lit by lights of various colours during the hourly musical guided tours; and the second is the **Castell Romà de Can Blai** (at the kilometre 10 mark on the way to La Mola), a Roman fort dating from the 3rd century AD which was originally built to safeguard the corn crop here. Naturally only the foundation walls remain of this large structure which once had five towers.

All the rough tracks on this promontory that run south and southwestwards lead to the long ★★ **Platja de Migjorn**, with its original beach bars. The various hotels and apartment buildings here have not made too negative an impression on the landscape.

To the west, beyond the Torre des Pi des Català, the Platja de Migjorn turns into the section of beach known as **Es Mal Pas**. Eastwards, at Es Arenals, the legendary beach bar, **Pirata Bus**, serves refreshments. It really was once an old bus flying pirate flags, but wind, sea and sand erosion finally finished the vehicle off. In the east, the Platja de Migjorn is dominated by the only large hotel complex on Formentera, the **Mar y Land** (or Maryland), and also the Club La Mola.

Along the coast on the northern side of the isthmus is the 5-km (3-mile) ★ **Platja de Tramuntana**, with the fishing harbour of Es Caló de Sant Agustí at its eastern end. The *tramuntana* winter wind, combined with the surf, has formed the rocks here into a bizarre coastal landscape.

The natural harbour of ★★ **Es Caló de Sant Agustí**, with its picturesque boathouses, has retained all the charm of a fishing village. This is further enhanced by the handful of restaurants and small family-run boarding houses. In Roman times, Es Caló was the most important harbour on the whole island.

Beyond Es Caló the road starts to wind its way up to the plateau of ★ **La Mola**, the highest point of which is **Sa Talaissa** (192m/630ft). The view at kilometre stone 14 is excellent, and takes in the entire flat part of the island, which is most of it. After that the road continues eastwards across the plateau in an almost straight line, as far as the **Far de la Mola** (lighthouse). Africa is just 250km (155 miles) away from here. Beyond the lighthouse, the dizzyingly steep cliffs fall away to the sea; the holes in the rocks serve as nesting places for numerous puffins (*virots*), which are now a protected species.

Thankfully, a traditional test of courage called *virotar* for young boys has now been stopped: eager to prove themselves, the boys used to lower themselves down from the clifftop on a rope and steal nesting birds from their

Roman Fort of Can Blai

Mar y Land

View to La Mola

perches. The puffins were then cooked over an open fire and eaten.

A memorial plaque beside the 130-year-old Far de la Mola commemorates the French author Jules Verne. It is uncertain whether he ever visited the island, but Hector Servadac, the hero of his *Voyage Through the Solar System*, began his interplanetary trip from the Mola plateau. Jules Verne certainly visited Mallorca, however, with his friend the Austrian archduke Ludwig Salvator. The latter could be termed Europe's first ever drop-out: he lived on Mallorca but travelled to Ibiza and Formentera, and recorded his impressions in a lengthy book on the Balearic Islands.

High noon in El Pilar

On the way back, stop at the village of ⋆ **El Pilar**. The simple church dates from the second half of the 18th century and is consecrated to the Mare de Déu del Pilar. However, on Sundays the local population doesn't only go to church – the main attraction of this tiny village is the little house belonging to the ceramic artist Gabrielet, covered with reeds and twigs and decorated with the bones of a whale that was once washed ashore here. Although the artist went back to Ibiza for reasons of age, the craft market he started at his bizarre workshop when he lived here still takes place every week.

Beyond El Pilar you can see Formentera's two best-preserved windmills. The rumour stubbornly persists that Bob Dylan lived in one of them, the **Moli Vell** (1778), during the 1960s.

Along the Roman Way

A very bumpy track leads past the windmills and off to the southwest to the only beach on La Mola: **S'Estufador** (6km/4 miles there and back, four-wheel drive only). After an adventurous descent there are a few boathouses built into the rocks – otherwise total solitude.

On the way back to the lower part of the island, the ⋆ **Camí Romà** (Roman Way) is a good place for a stroll: it's a partly cobbled but very weathered path that branches off to the right of the main road before the hairpin section and continues in an almost straight line through the forest, until it reaches the main road again at Mar y Land. This route, which features one of the finest views on Formentera, is also known as the *Camí des Frares*, because it was used by the Augustinian friars who once lived in the now-ruined monastery of Es Monestir on La Mola.

Capella sa Tanca Vella

Around 9km (5 miles) further along the main road is ⋆⋆⋆ **Sant Francesç Xavier**, the capital of Formentera. Although of modest size, it does have several sights: the ⋆ **Capella sa Tanca Vella**, for instance, a small stone chapel with a barrel vault which dates from the 14th century. The fortified church of Església de Sant Francesç

Xavier became the more important religious structure in 1726, and was sometimes even provided with cannon. It has a long and relatively high nave, and some interesting Moorish-style ornamentation on its cemetery wall.

Sant Francesç has a private ★ **Museu Etnologic** (daily 10am–2pm), where exhibits include a salt-pan locomotive. Originally housed inside the restaurant of the Deportivo sports club, the museum is now located at c/Sant Jaume I, 17.

From Sant Francesç it's only another 7km (4 miles) or so to the quietest part of the island, with its extreme southwestern point, the ★★★ **Cap de Barbària**. The route passes a few hills, the highest of which is Puig d'en Guillem (107m/350ft). The only holiday resort in the southwestern part of the island is situated on the picturesque, forest-lined sandy bay of **Cala Saona**.

The route to the lighthouse **Far des Cap de Barbària** is lined by several remote *fincas* with sheep grazing around them. Farmer's wives can sometimes be seen spinning wool on bobbins; this later gets turned into soft Formentera wool pullovers, which can be seen hanging at the various street stalls for sale.

Roughly 2km (1 mile) before the Cap de Barbària, the stone wall of **Tanca d'Allà Dins** divides off the southernmost tip of the island. Beyond it lie the ruins of Formentera's second megalithic site, **Cap de Barbària II** (on the road to Sant Francesç after the Cap de Barbària). In the 4,000 years or so that separate this settlement from the present day, the land has only been affected by wind, sun and sea. One lighthouse and also a watchtower, the **Torre d'es Garroveret** (the best-preserved of Formentera's five pirate towers), are the only man-made structures in an otherwise totally natural landscape.

Breezy day at Cap de Barbària

Sant Francesç locals

Art and Architecture

Architecture

The landscape of Ibiza is distinctive for its innumerable stone walls enclosing fields and gardens, and the dazzlingly white traditional farmhouses (*ses cases*), which are always made up of several cubic sections.

The simple architecture has an aesthetic function, making the best possible use of materials available on the island: natural stone, the hard wood of the Phoenician juniper, clay and limestone. This elementary building style has fascinated numerous 20th-century architects and designers such as Le Corbusier, Walter Gropius, Erwin Broner, Raoul Hausmann and other Bauhaus exponents. They saw this 'architecture without architects' as a realisation and a confirmation of their aim for functional simplicity: the small windows in the 1.5-m (5-ft) thick walls kept houses cool in summer and warm in winter, as well as letting in light; and the design was not only in harmony with human needs but also the surrounding landscape.

Tourism changed all of this. The old harmony of architecture and landscape has mostly disappeared, and much of the construction work is dictated by time and cost, with buildings generally made of precast concrete slabs. The simple furnishings of old have also been largely replaced by bourgeois and often pretentious interiors.

Painting

The soft, warm light on Ibiza and Formentera, the gentle landscape and the mild climate have long exerted a strong influence on artists. Ibiza has had a widely respected art gallery since as long ago as the 1940s, with exhibits by local figurative painters such as Antoni 'Portmany' Mari (1906–74) and Narcis Puget (1874–1960). They were gradually joined by such avant-garde painters as Will Faber (1901–90) and Erwin Broner (1898–71).

During the 1950s, there were several innovative influences. At that time, numerous foreign artists arrived on the islands, which had an effect on the growing number of local painters. In 1959, the so-called Group '59, composed of eight foreigners and one Spaniard, brought Ibiza international recognition. Today a number of important artists still live on Ibiza and Formentera, among them Erwin Bechtold (born in Cologne 1925, founder member of Group '59), Emilio Vedova (born in Venice 1919), Barry Flanagan (born in Wales 1941) and native artists Tur Costa (born 1927) and Paco Romero (born 1966).

The lively competition between the various discotheques on Ibiza has resulted in a very inventive 'poster' art. Graffiti has also become something of a subculture, adding interest to otherwise featureless concrete walls.

Opposite: Church of Sant Domènec, Eivissa

The church at Sant Vicenç de sa Cala

Simple but effective

Gypsy dance in progress

Music and Dance

The stars of the Ibiza music scene are the DJs, some of whom are well known and are often booked for international raves and similar events. As well as several famous composers and performers who live on the islands, several local pop and rock groups, such as *Estatuas de Sal* and *Los Desperfectos*, are gradually making a name for themselves on mainland Spain.

Sax appeal

Ibiza and Formentera, however, can look back on thousands of years of musical tradition with roots dating back to the Phoenician and Moorish periods. Typical early instruments included a four-holed flute (*flauta*) made of oleander, a drum (*tambor*) made of pine and goatskin and also a metal rapier beaten with a stick (*espasí*). They accompany performances of the *cantades pagesas*, or 'farmers' songs', and also the unusual and enjoyable folk dances, or flamenco, on the islands. The *cantades pagesas* are improvised chants sung in guttural tones that tell stories and usually provide a humorous glimpse into the respective singer's philosophy of life. Folk performances often include songs involving both men and women known as *cancons de porfedi*, or 'argument songs', despite their usually harmonious content.

Such traditions have been researched by the musicians Joan Mureno and Isidor Marí, whose *Trio UC* can often be heard performing at folk festivals. Every Thursday at 6pm you can experience folk dancing in the churchyard in Sant Miquel de Balansat.

Otherwise, dancing and music is in abundance at any of the village festivals held during the late summer. All the main parishes hold *Nits d'Estiu* ('Summer Nights'), when classical and traditional music and dancing takes place in the open air.

Folk dance

Festivals and Folklore

January
On the eve of Epiphany, the procession of the *Reyos Magos* (Three Kings) is held in Eivissa. It begins at the harbour because according to legend the kings originally came from across the seas. On 17 January, the festival of St Anthony is celebrated in Sant Antoni; the farmers bring their animals to be blessed and then have a big festival.

February
Carnivals held in Eivissa, Sant Antoni and Santa Eulàlia. The patron saint St Eulàlia is celebrated on 12 February.

March
Festival of St José (Catalan *Josep*) on 12 March (also Father's Day) with biggest celebrations in Sant Josep.

April
Good Friday procession in medieval costume in Eivissa marks the start of *Semana Santa* (Holy Week). St George's Day on 23 April marks not only the village festival in Sant Jordi de Ses Salines but also Literature Day.

May
The *Rocio* flower festival on the first Sunday in the month is a real eye-opener, with a large procession of flower-bedecked carts.

June
Nit de Sant Joan (St John's Night) on 23 June: massive effigies are burnt on Ibiza and Formentera. The village festival of Sant Joan is held on the following day with music, dancing and fireworks.

July
The Virgen de Carmen, patron saint of fishermen and seafarers, is commemorated on 16 July. The boat processions in Eivissa and Sant Antoni are followed by folk festivals.

August
The festival in honour of the Pitiusas' patron saint, Santa Maria de las Nieves (St Mary of the Snows), is held on 5 August on both islands. Events include music, dancing and sports, as well as a firework display. Reconquest Day is celebrated on 8 August – also the day of Sant Ciriac, Eivissa's patron saint.

September
Music and dancing take place in several villages around the old community fountains. These fountain festivals date back to the pre-Christian era, and were probably an early form of rain dance. Andalusians also have their own week-long festival, the *Feria Andaluza*, in Eivissa.

December
The start of the month is marked by the wine festival of Sant Mateu, where new wine and Cava can be sampled. 28 December is *Los Santos Innocentes* (Innocent Children's Day), the Spanish equivalent of April Fool's Day.

Animals are blessed

Holy Week

Reconquest Day is on 8 August

LA OLIVA

Food and Drink

Tourism has changed the islands' former eating habits out of all recognition. At weekends the locals now tend to favour the numerous restaurants run by foreigners that have been springing up everywhere since the late 1960s. The selection is highly international – from French, Italian, German and Swedish to Mexican and Moroccan. The Orient is represented by Chinese, Japanese, Indian and Vietnamese establishments.

Despite this, the genuine and typical local food still changes with the seasons. The *truita amb esparrecs* (omelette with wild asparagus) is only served during the winter, and *guisat de caragols* (a snail dish) during the rainy season along with mushrooms. *Cuinat*, a delicious mix of cabbage, beans and peas, is cooked during Lent.

For all traditional dishes on Ibiza and Formentera, the same applies: 'The best ingredient for a meal is plenty of time.' One basic is *sofrit*: onions, tomatoes and garlic are fried briefly in olive oil and then enriched with combinations of parsley, green pepper or bay leaves as required. This base is then used in risottos, stews or soups. If skate is added to the *sofrit* together with almonds, lemon and egg, it results in Ibiza's famous *burrida de ratjada*. Various kinds of fish mixed with saffron, almonds and potatoes turn the *sofrit* into a *guisat de peix*; and if different types of sausage and meat are added, it becomes a *sofrit pagès*.

Important ingredients of this uncomplicated but very filling local cuisine include fish, mutton, chicken and especially pork, plus a large variety of vegetables and beans. The food is rather less filling in the summer months, when salads tend to be the preferred choice.

At Easter time the locals serve *flaó*, a cake with a mint-flavoured topping consisting of fresh ewe's cheese, sugar and eggs. At Christmas every household has its *salsa*, a thick sauce made from chicken stock, grated almonds, honey, peppers and blood sausage, into which large pieces of bread are dunked.

The islanders generally like to drink a dry red wine which some might consider a little too sour. A slightly sweeter version, *Sa Cova* (red, white and rosé), can be obtained either at Sant Mateu where it is made or at certain *bodegas* (wine taverns). Ibiza's famous herbal liqueurs are very popular as desserts or as digestifs; two well-known ones are *Hierbas Ibicencas* and *Frigola*, and get served ice cold in the summer. Cognac is popular in the winter, and is often served alight in the glass (*coñac caliente*).

A typical coffee variant on Ibiza is *café caleta*, which is also very popular at outdoor barbecues (*torradas*):

Opposite: tempting sign in Eivissa

Enjoy a sea view

Sausages

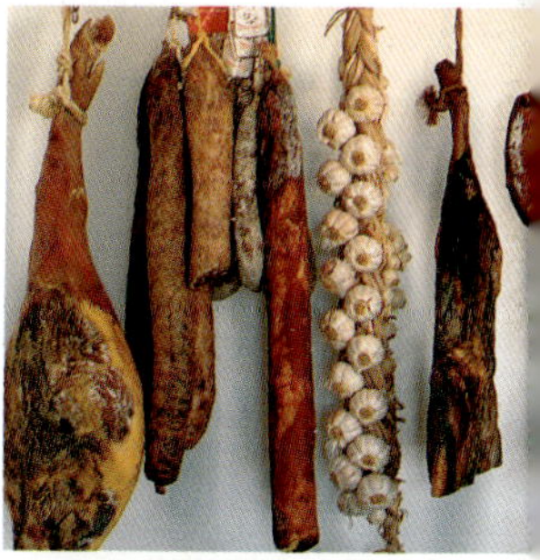

Herbal liqueurs

ground coffee and whole coffee beans are cooked in water over an open fire and then flavoured with lemon, cinnamon, sugar and cognac.

The complete meal

Al fresco in Eivissa

Restaurant selection

Here is a list of some restaurants on Ibiza and Formentera. $$$ means expensive, $$ medium-priced and $ cheap.

Ibiza

Cala de Sant Vicenç

$Restaurante Mari, Cala de Sant Vicenç. Has a small garden and serves delicious meat and seafood dishes.

Eivissa

$$$El Faro, Placa de Sa Riba 2–1, tel: 31 32 33. Elegant restaurant with a view across the harbour; paella and fresh seafood. **$$Can Alfredo**, Passeig Vara de Rey 16, tel: 31 12 74. Traditional restaurant with Ibizan cuisine, frequented by local intellectuals. **$$La Plaza**, Placa de Vila 18, tel: 30 76 17. Small but very good restaurant in the historic upper town, with French and German specialities. **$$Formentera**, C de Lluis Tur i Palau 4, tel 31 10 24. Comfortable restaurant opposite the harbour office. **$Bar Sport**, C Comte de Rosselló. Beneath the arcades of the Montesol, very simple but very good food and friendly service. **$Comidas San Juan**, C Montgrí, tel: 31 07 63. Tiny, family-run establishment specialising in Ibizan cuisine.

Portinatx

$$Es Caliú, on the road to Portinatx, km 10, tel: 33 13 68. In an old farmhouse, specialises in grilled meat.

Sant Antoni de Portmany

$$$Can Pujol, on the old road to Port des Torrent, tel: 34 14 07. Famed for its delicious local food and fish, and pleasantly uncomplicated. **$Es Rebost de Can Prats**, C Cervantes 4, tel: 34 62 52. Delicious local food that tends to take rather a long time to arrive.

Sant Josep de Sa Talaia

$$$Ca'n Domingo de Ca'n Botja, Ctra Sant Josep, km 9, tel: 80 01 84. Remote and romantic in a renovated farmhouse serving primarily local cuisine. **$$$Ca Na Joana**, Ctra Sant Josep, km 10, tel: 80 01 58. Owned by a former journalist who serves imaginative food and often talks about her meeting with The Beatles.

Sant Mateu d'Aubarca

$$La Plaza, Placa de l'Església, tel: 19 70 75. Eat on a terrace set in a luxuriant park. French cuisine.

Sant Miquel
$Can Cameta, C de l'Església, tel: 33 10 37. Relax on a leafy terrace and eat home-made pasta.

Sant Rafel de Sa Creu
$$Clodenis, next to the church, tel: 19 85 45. Restaurant inside a former grocery store, serving Provençal cuisine. **$Sa Creu**, Isidor Macabich 13, tel: 19 80 61. Simple, wholesome home cooking.

Santa Agnès
$Can Cosmi, on the square in front of the church, tel: 80 50 20. This restaurant serves the best *tortilla española* (Spanish omelette) on the island. Seats are on a high terrace with a wonderful view.

Santa Eulària des Riu
$$.Ca Na Ribes, C Sant Jaume 67, tel: 33 00 06. Ibizan and international specialities in served in a pretty courtyard. **$El Pinchito**, C San Vicenç 36. Simple, family-run restaurant.

Ses Salines
$$Malibú, Platja de Ses Salines. Beach restaurant , where food can be taken to yachts by boat. **$$Cap des Falcó**, 18 74 76. Great seafood by the sea.

Formentera

Es Caló
$$Can Rafalet, Fonda Rafalet, tel: 908-13 65 92 (mobile). Restaurant with overnight accommodation by the sea, and, of course, specialising in a wide range of seafood.

Es Pujols
$$Sa Palmera, S'Aigua Dolca 15-31, tel: 32 83 56. Large and simple restaurant with typical local dishes, the seafood is especially good.

Platja de Ses Illetes
$$$Es Molí de Sal, Platja de Ses Illetes, tel: 18 74 91. Inside an old salt mill; serves excellent fish and rice dishes.

Sant Ferran de ses Roques
$$La Tortuga, on the main road at the turn-off to Es Ca Mari (roughly 1km/0.6 miles outside Sant Ferran), located inside a former *tienda* (grocery shop).

Sant Francesç
$Bar Estrella Dorada, next to the Town Hall. Their delicious *tapas* are extremely popular with locals and visitors alike.

Fish specialities

The Estrella Dorada

Sant Antoni in full swing

Nightlife

Ibiza is notorious for its nightlife with a large proportion of visitors coming to the island solely to go clubbing. Mostly around Sant Antoni and Eivissa, bars, often with live music, start opening in the afternoon and fill up before the nightclubs open at around midnight. One club, Space, offers daytime clubbing. DJs from BBC Radio One take up residence in the summer.

Ibiza Trips offers a special nightclubbers' package *(see page 71)*, but bar and club crawls are organised by other operators as well. Here is a small selection of what's on offer:

The latest sounds

El Divino

Bars

Cafe del Mar, on seafront in Sant Antoni; 6pm–4am. *The* place to see the sunset. **Mambo Cafe**, on seafront in Sant Antoni; 11am– 4am. Attracts the 'beautiful' people. Resident DJ, live music and serves food. **Bar M**, Sant Antoni near Es Paradis; 4pm–4am. Pre-club parties and food.

Clubs

Pacha, Avda. 8 de Agosto, Eivissa; tel: 31 36 12; 9.30pm–5am; 1,000 capacity. Reputed to be one of the most beautiful clubs in the world. Attracts jetsetters. **Amnesia**, Sant Rafael; tel: 19 80 41; midnight–7am; 4,000 capacity. Foam parties a speciality. **Privilège** (ex KU), Sant Rafael; tel: 19 80 70; midnight–7am; 7,000 capacity. Top-class clubbing in luxury surroundings. Manumission night is on Thursday. **El Divino**, Port Esportíu Ibiza Nueva; tel: 19 01 76; 9.30pm–3am. Attracts the yachties. **Es Paradis**, Sant Antoni; tel: 34 34 12; 11.30pm–6am. Water parties. **Space**, end of airport runway; tel: 30 69 90; 6am–8pm.

Active Holidays

Golf

The Club de Golf Ibiza at Roca Llisa (8km/5 miles from Eivissa) is set in a magnificent landscape with a beautiful sea view. A bigger course (27 holes) with full facilities, the Golf de Ibiza, is located nearby at Santa Eulària (8km/5miles out on the road to Jesús).

Hiking and Cycling

The best way to discover the beauty of the Ibizan landscape is to hike through it, while Formentera's flat terrain is ideal for cycling. The Consell Insular and various municipalities have been trying to promote these activities for years now, and hiking and cycling maps are available from tourist offices (*see page 73*).

Horse-riding

A lot of Ibizans are crazy about horses, and the biggest excitement is betting at the trap-racing courses in Sant Rafel and Sant Jordi. Many hotels and riding stables organise riding lessons and excursions, such as Can Mayans (tel: 18 73 88) in Santa Gertrudis, and the Can Sires stables (tel. 34 15 54) just outside Sant Antoni, run by an Englishwoman. Las Cuadras d'Ibiza stables (tel: 19 70 11) are behind the Pachá disco in Eivissa.

Windsurfing off Ses Salines

Watersports

Of Ibiza's 50 or so beaches, only two are jam-packed in the summertime: the Platja de Ses Salines and the Platja d'en Bossa. Both are southwest of Eivissa and are popular not only because of their proximity to the capital but also because of their fine sand, gentle slopes and large size. There are two official nudist beaches on Ibiza (Aigues Blanques and the Platja de Es Cavallet), and one on Formentera (Ses Illetes).

Nude divers at Aigues Blanques

Many beaches have water skiing, pedal-boating and surfing facilities and several offer sailing lessons and boat hire as do the four sports harbours in Ibiza (three in the Bay of Eivissa, and one near Sant Antoni), and the Club La Mola on Formentera. Aquaparks also provide excellent and safe family entertainment, e.g. the Aguamar on the Platja d'en Bossa and Aqualandia at Cap Martinet.

Diving centres are well equipped

The numerous small rocky coves to the north and west of Ibiza are only visited by those in the know. You may find a quiet corner there, and the crystal-clear waters and fascinating marine life make the area highly popular with divers. There are diving centres in Sant Antoni, Cala Vedella, Portinatx and Port de Sant Miquel.

A detailed list of watersports centres and schools on Ibiza is given in the annual brochure *Turismo*.

Getting There

Opposite: in the alleys of Eivissa

By plane

In the summer a whole host of travel companies offer package holidays or direct charter flights to Ibiza at competitive prices. If you already have accommodation on either of the islands, it is advisable to shop around for the best charter flight deal via Teletext, the weekend newspapers or your local travel agent. Flying time direct from the UK to Ibiza is around two hours. To get to Formentera, fly to Ibiza and continue by ferry (*see page* 72).

Easy directions

Companies operating to Ibiza and Formentera include: Airtours, tel: 0870-608 1955, fax: 0870-161 6166; Thomson Holidays, tel: 0870-550 2555, fax: 0141-429 6761; First Choice Holidays, tel: 0161-745 7000, fax: 0161-745 4533; JMC, tel: 0870-607 5085, fax: 01274-387 740; Unijet Travel, tel: 0990-336 336. These companies are all members of ABTA (Association of British Travel agents) and ATOL (Air Travel Organisers Licence).

Ibiza Trips, tel: 020-7836 1414, fax: 020-7240 0445, offers a special nightclubbers' package which includes flight, accommodation, transfers and supplements plus passes to three clubs (Manumission, Space and one of your choice). It is a member of ABTA (Association of British Travel agents) and ATOL (Air travel Organisers Licence).

Scheduled flights operate every day from Britain and involve a change of plane in Barcelona or Madrid. They are more expensive than charter but the advantage is that you can go more or less when you choose.

Iberian Airlines, tel: 020-7830 0011 (national reservation number for London and Manchester). Change planes at Barcelona.

British Airways, tel: 0345-222111 (Linkline), flies from Gatwick to Barcelona where you change to Iberian Airlines to Ibiza.

Trasmediterránea arrival

By ferry

Anyone travelling by car, bus or train travels as far as Barcelona, Denia or Valencia, and takes the car ferry from there to Ibiza. Several boats a day leave Denia for Ibiza and Formentera, even in winter time, and the crossing takes roughly four hours. From Barcelona ferries leave daily in the summer, and three times a week in the winter; the trip can take between 8 and 9 hours, depending on the weather.

You can book in the UK through **Trasmediterránea** c/o Southern Ferries, 1st Floor, 179 Piccadilly, London W1V 9DB; tel: 020-7491 4968, fax: 020-7491 3502.

Getting Around

Inter-island ferry

By ferry

There are ferry connections almost hourly between Ibiza and Formentera. Crossing on the car ferry, which leaves three times a day, takes one hour; the faster boats take just 20 minutes. Information on arrival and departure times can be obtained at the Formentera quay, Avinguda Santa Eulària, Eivissa. Small excursion boats also dock at the harbour in Sant Antoni and travel to the bays to the north and south of the town; in Santa Eulària, excursions are also possible to Tagomago island and Formentera.

By bus

The main towns on Ibiza and several very attractive beaches can be reached by bus. The main route between Eivissa and Sant Antoni is serviced by one bus line that runs every 15 minutes on weekdays from 7.30am–11.30pm, and then once an hour until 5am. On Sundays and public holidays it only runs half-hourly during the day. The bus to Santa Eulària travels at similar intervals. Bus connections to other locations on Ibiza are not always favourable, so it's best to check a timetable first, available from hotels and the tourist office.

Heading upcountry

By taxi

The taxis on Ibiza don't have meters, so always ask about the price before you leave. The driver has to have an official price list, and show it on request. If you're headed for a country house in the middle of nowhere, be prepared to be dropped off somewhat earlier and to walk along a bumpy track by yourself.

By car or bicycle

If you want to explore the island on your own, cars, motorcycles, bicycles or mopeds are all available for hire at the airport or in any hotel area. The minimum age for car hire is 21. Bicycles are especially recommended during the summer, when cars without air conditioning can turn into ovens. By the way, be very careful when overtaking: if a car travelling in front of you switches on its left indicator, it is not necessarily intending to turn left or overtake – the message can also mean 'Be careful, there's someone in front of me planning to turn left'.

For motoring in Ibiza and Formentera, an EU format Driving Licence is accepted or an International Driving Licence available from the AA or RAC. If you are travelling in your own car, the vehicle log book/registration are required. Third party insurance is compulsory; you can obtain a Green Card from your insurance company.

On-the-spot payment of fines is compulsory.

Information in Eivissa

Facts for the Visitor

Entry regulations

As Ibiza and Formentera are a part of Spain, visitors from the European Union just need a full passport to enter the country. EU, Norway and Iceland passport holders do not need visas, but for stays over 90 days require a residence permit. Passport holders from the US, Japan and Canada only need a visa for a stay of longer than 90 days.

Customs

Since 1993, no duty has been payable on goods for personal use taken out of the country to other European destinations. The guidelines here per person are roughly 800 cigarettes and 10 litres of spirits.

Tourist information

In the UK: Spanish Tourist Office, 22/23 Manchester Square, London W1M 5AP; tel: 020-7486 8077; fax: 020-7486 8034.

In the US: Tourist Office of Spain, 666 5th Avenue, 35th Floor, New York, NY10103; tel: 212-265 8822; fax: 212-265 8864; 8383 Wilshire Boulevard, Suite 960, Beverly Hills, CA90211; tel: 323-658 7188; fax: 323-658 1061.

Information centres on Ibiza: Sant Antoni, Passeig de ses Fonts, tel. 34 33 63; Eivissa, Avda. Espanya 49, tel: 30 19 00; Santa Eulària, C. Mariano Riquer Wallis 4, tel. 33 07 28. On Formentera: La Savina, tel. 32 20 57.

A place for pesetas

Money

The unit of currency in Spain is the peseta (Pta.). Bank notes of 1000, 2000, 5000 and 10000 pesetas are in circulation, as are coins worth 1, 5, 10, 25, 100, 200 and 500 pesetas. Money is available outside banking hours from automatic credit card cash dispensers, and many

Ceramics and shawls

shops also accept plastic money. Eurocheques are best cashed at banks, where the exchange rates are also usually more favourable than at travel agents or exchange outlets.

Souvenirs

The many small markets (*mercadillos*) on Ibiza and Formentera are the best place to buy souvenirs. These include hats made of straw, shoes made of cloth and straw, miniature clay houses and also copies of Phoenician terracotta figurines. Herbal liqueurs such as *Hierbas ibicencas* or *Frigola* are also very popular. More expensive are filigree gold and silver jewellery, or hand-made ceramics.

Opening times

These vary, but shops are generally open from 9am–2pm and 4–9pm. Boutiques open late in the morning but also close a lot later as well (sometimes at midnight). Supermarkets such as Syp and Hipercentro open from 10am–10pm Monday to Saturday. Small shops in rural areas open as early as 8am.

Public holidays

1 January (New Year's Day), 6 January (Epiphany), Maundy Thursday and Good Friday, 1 May (Labour Day), 25 July (Spanish National Day), 5 August (Pitiusas name day celebrations), 15 August (Ascension), 12 October (Spanish Day), 1 November (All Saints' Day), 6 December (Constitution Day), 8 December (Immaculate Conception), 25 December (Christmas).

Time

Ibiza and Formentera are on CET (Central European Time), so they're usually one hour ahead of the UK. Spain also has summertime and wintertime.

Poste haste

Tipping

In restaurants 5–10 percent of the price is normal as a tip. Porters, doormen, chambermaids, bus drivers and tour guides should all be tipped at least 100 pesetas for their pains. With cab drivers, simply round off the official sum.

Postal services

The same price of 65 pta applies to postcards and ordinary letters to all European destinations. Post offices are open Monday to Saturday from 9am–2pm, and in Eivissa from 8.30am–8pm except Saturday afternoon. Stamps can also be purchased from *estancos* (tobacconists).

Telephones

Calls can be made abroad from all phones on the island, with 100 pta coins, or phonecards. Instructions in your language are available. Calls are cheaper between 10pm and 8am and from 2pm on Saturday until 8am on Monday. The dialling code for the UK is 0044. To call Ibiza or Formentera from abroad, dial 0034 for Spain and the local code: 971.

Electricity

220V almost everywhere. Adaptors are required.

Clothing

Although the local saying '*Vistete como quieras*' (wear what you want) applies on the islands, don't walk through the streets in swimwear. Tops must be worn in buses (this applies to men too). The sun is strong, so bring high-factor sun cream and hats, and wear T-shirts for protection.

Sun hats and shorts

Nudism

Ibiza has two official nudist beaches at Es Cavallet and Aigues Blanques; the one on Formentera is at Ses Illetes. Nudism is common at numerous remote bays and coves without bars or restaurants, however, and going topless has become more of a fashion issue than a moral one.

Medical assistance

Hospitals, medical centres and private practices are dotted across the whole island. First aid and more is provided by the Red Cross's *Casa de Socorro*, tel: 30 12 14, or the hospital of Can Misses, Barrio Can Misses, tel: 39 70 00. Medical centres, called *Centros Médicos,* with multilingual staff are also located all over Ibiza, tel: 34 00 00.

On Formentera contact the *Consultorio Médico*, Ctra La Savina, tel: 32 03 56, for medical assistance. There is also a doctor on 24-hour standby duty, tel: 32 28 91.

Take out health insurance before travelling. If you are from the EU, medical care is free with an E111 form which you must get before leaving home.

Pharmacies

These are called *farmacias*, and can be recognised by the green cross. For ones that open outside business hours, look in the local paper under *farmacias de guardia.*

Emergency

Dial 112 for ambulance, fire brigade and police; also available in English.

Diplomatic representation

British Consulates: Avenida Isidoro Macabich 45, 1st Floor, 07800 Eivissa; tel: 30 18 18; Placa Mayor 3d, 07002 Palma de Mallorca.

American Consulate: Avenida Jaime III, 26 Entresuelo, 07012 Palma de Mallorca; tel: 72 50 51.

Apartment-style accommodation in Sant Eulària

Accommodation

Beyond the skyscrapers

Several individual offers are available alongside the usual package holiday accommodation on both Ibiza and Formentera. Instead of getting claustrophobic in a mini-Manhattan, why not try out a house or a *finca* (farm) out in the countryside, or a nice family-run boarding house where children are welcome?

Idyllically situated country hotels provide a pleasant alternative to the large ones right beside the sea, although staying in these places can admittedly be expensive (they often charge double the package offer, even if the rating is no more than three stars). What you do get, however, is rural peace and quiet, a unique landscape, and personal service. Some of these hotels are only marked as *hostals*, i.e. they're roughly equivalent to a *hotel garni* (breakfast only). A full list of all the available accommodation possibilities can be obtained from tourist information offices (*see page 73*).

Talamanca hotelscape

Categories of accommodation

Normal hotels (H) offer full board and lodging on request; apartment hotels (HA) provide self-catering facilities in a holiday apartment; a Hotel Residencia (HR) offers half-board and has its own restaurant where lunchtime and evening meals are served; there is also a choice from the à la carte if desired. A Hostal (Hs) is a boarding house that provides breakfast in with the price of the accommodation, whereas a Hostal Residencia (HsR) is a boarding house with a restaurant. In a Residencia Apartamentos (RA) you can cater for yourself or eat à la carte in an adjoining restaurant. A Casa Huéspedes (CH) is a guest house providing only overnight accommodation. Finally, there's the Fonda (F), which is rather like a country inn, where meals and accommodation are billed for separately.

Hotels, apartment hotels and holiday clubs (Ciudad de Vacaciones, CV) usually close down in the winter.

Finca holidays

These holidays in remote farmhouses in the interior are very pleasant, but also virtually impossible to arrange officially through travel agents. The usual way of finding a *finca* to spend a summer in is to ask friends on the island to organise one in the springtime, or to check the newspapers at home for advertisements.

Camping

Camping out anywhere in the countryside other than on an official campsite is forbidden on both Ibiza and Formentera. Ibiza has seven campsites, including the ones in Es Canyar, Cala Bassa and near Sant Antoni. They are divided up into three categories according to the Spanish system, with 'I' as the lowest. Attempts at setting up a site on Formentera have so far failed because of hostility from environmentalists.

Hotel selection

Here is a list of some hotels and campsites to be found on Ibiza and Formentera. $$$ means expensive, $$ medium-priced and $ cheap.

Ibiza

Cala Llonga

$Apartamentos Los Albatros, tel: 33 95 80. A good place for people who like booking their own accommodation. **Camping Cala Llonga**, category I, tel: 33 21 19. Five minutes from the beach, on a terraced slope under shady pine trees, with a restaurant, a bar and a swimming pool.

Cala Mastella

Camping Cala Nova, category II, tel: 33 17 74. Under some nice shady evergreens, tents can be rented, and the beach is 45m (50yds) away.

Eivissa

$$$El Palacio, C Conquesta 2, tel: 30 14 78, fax: 39 15 81, Small hotel in an old house in the Vila Mitjana with a view across the town, plus a pool and romantic grounds, and the interior design has been largely inspired by movie greats such as Marilyn Monroe, Charlie Chaplin, etc. **$$$La Ventana** (HsR), Sa Carossa 13, tel: 39 08 57, fax: 39 01 45. Small town hotel with French cuisine, located just below the Santa Llucia bastion. **$$$Ocean Drive**,

El Palacio and El Corsario

Marina Botafoc, tel: 31 22 22, fax: 31 22 28. All rooms in this hotel run by Nicki Lauda are noise insulated. **$$Montesol**, Passeig Vara de Rey 2, tel: 31 01 61. The oldest hotel in town, built in Spanish colonial style in 1930 and renovated in the early 1990s, very central. **$La Marina**, C Barcelona 7, tel: 31 01 72. Family-run establishment with restaurant, right next to the harbour. **$Parque**, Placa del Parque, tel: 30 13 58. Quiet boarding house located conveniently close to the centre of town.

Platja de Ses Salines
$Hostal Sa Palmera, Ses Salines, tel: 908-63 08 38 (mobile). A popular boarding house for those who prefer peace and quiet, being near the sea and far away from the massive hotel complexes.

Platja d'en Bossa
$$Los Molinos, C Ramón Muntaner 60, tel: 30 25 50. A four-star hotel idyllically located right next to the sea, with a fantastic view of Formentera.

Portinatx
Camping Payés, category III, tel: 33 31 14. A campsite with a playground and friendly staff who ensure that children feel at home, so parents can relax. There's also a cheap restaurant.

Pike's (above) and Paradise Stella Maris

Sant Agustí d'Es Vedrà
$$$Victoria, Ctra Cala Tarida, Sant Agustí, tel: 34 09 00. A small hotel high up on a hill with a great view of the west coast.

Sant Antoni de Portmany
$$$Pike's, Camino Sa Vorera, km 12, tel: 34 22 22, fax: 34 23 12. Luxury *finca* hotel which not only sells comfort but also lifestyle, and whose guests have included such luminaries as Grace Jones, Freddy Mercury and Harrison Ford. **$$Paradise Stella Maris**, Ctra Cap Negret, tel: 34 06 00, fax: 34 27 31. A holiday club with plenty of sports facilities including tennis, volleyball, boccia, swimming pool, minigolf etc., open to residents and non-residents alike. **$Rita**, C Mallorca 5–7, tel: 34 01 68. A quiet *hostal* outside the town centre with over 27 rooms of average standard. **Camping Cala Bassa**, category II, tel: 34 45 99. 500m (¼ mile) from the beach and 10km (6 miles) out of Sant Antoni.

Sant Joan de l'Abritja
$Ca'n Pla Roig, on the main street, tel: 33 30 12. A pretty boarding house on the edge of the village with a good view, open all year round.

Sant Josep de Sa Talaia
$$$Jardins de Palerm, tel: 80 01 76. Idyllically situated in an old farmhouse, at the highest point of the village.

Sant Miquel
$$$Hacienda, Na Xamena, Sant Miquel, tel: 33 45 00, fax: 33 45 14. The only five-star hotel on Ibiza, where the jetsetters go, very majestically situated on the edge of Cap Balansat.

Santa Eulària des Riu
$$$Cas Catala, Calle del Sol, tel: 33 10 06. Small hotel with 12 rooms, ideal for those seeking peace and quiet. **$$$La Posada**, Puig de Missa, tel: 33 00 17. In an old farmhouse in a picturesque landscape. **$$Tres Torres**, Ses Estaques, tel: 33 03 26. Large establishment just outside town which exhibits the work of local artists in the summertime. **$Hostal Rey**, C San Josep 17, tel: 33 02 10. Centrally located just behind the Town Hall, family atmosphere. **Camping Florida**, category III, Punta Arabí, tel: 33 16 98. Underneath some shady trees right next to the sea, perfect for families; **Camping Es Canà**, category I. Just 10 minutes from the beach, with a bar, restaurant and swimming pool.

Santa Eulària

Formentera

Cala Saona
$$Hostal Cala Saona, tel: 32 20 30, fax: 32 25 09. Just 45m (50yds) from a fantastic beach, with a park, a pool and a playground.

Es Caló de Sant Agustí
$Miramar, Es Caló, 32 70 60. Family-run establishment on the main street. The lady owners knit Formentera woolly pullovers, and mopeds are hired out opposite.

Es Pujols
$$Roca Bella, Platja Es Pujols, tel: 32 81 30, fax: 32 80 02. This was the first hotel to be built on Formentera (1957) and still has the charm of those early days. **$Hostal Residencia Mayans**, tel: 32 87 24. In the centre of Es Pujols, so rather noisy, but has a friendly family atmosphere.

Platja de Migjorn
$Hostal Maysi, Platja de Migjorn, Es Arenals, tel: 32 85 47. Just a few steps away from the beach, where surfboards and pedalboats can be hired.
$Hostal Illes Pitiüses, tel: 32 81 89, fax: 32 80 17. Clean rooms and exceptionally friendly staff.

Index

Accommodation......76–9
administration..........11
Aigues Blanques........48
Aqualandia..............49
architecture.............61

Balàfia....................46
Bar Anita.................52
bars.......................68

Ca na Costa
 megalithic tomb....55–6
Cala Carbó...............36
Cala Comte...............41
Cala d'Hort...............36
Cala de Sant Vicenç....48
Cala des Moltó...........43
Cala Jondal...............34
Cala Llonga...............50
Cala Mastella.............52
Cala Salada...............40
Cala Vedella..............37
Cala Xarraca..............47
Camí Romà
 (Roman Way)...........58
camping...................77
Can Pujol museum......39
Cap de Barbària and
 megalithic site.........59
Cap Martinet..............49
Cap Negret................40
Castell
 Romà de Can Blai....57
climate......................7
clubs.......................68
Cova d'en Xeroni........57
Cova des Vi................40
Cova Santa................34
cuisine.....................65
customs..............8–10
cycling.................69, 72

Dance.......................62

Economy.............10–11
Eivissa...............16–28
 Ajuntament...............25
 Almudaina................24
 Antic Seminaria.........25
 Baluard de
 Sant Bernat............24
 Capella de
 Sant Ciriac.............22
 Carrer de la
 Santa Creu.........21–2
 Carrer de la Verge....20
 cathedral.................24
 El Corsario Hotel......25
 Es Calvari.................24
 Es Castell.................24
 Es Mercat Vell...........20
 Es Polvorí...........25–6
 Església del
 Hospitalet..............22
 Església
 Sant Domènec.........25
 Església Sant Elm.....20
 Far de Batafoc..........28
 Montesol Hotel..........27
 Monument a
 Vara de Rey............27
 Monument
 al Corsaris..............18
 Museu Arqueològic..23
 Museu d'Art
 Contemporani.........26
 Passeig de Moll........28
 Passeig Maritim........28
 Passeig Vara de Rey.27
 Plaça de la Catedral..23
 Plaça de la Vila.........21
 Plaça de Sa Font...20–1
 Platja des Duros........28
 Portal Nou................22
 Portal de ses Taules..21
 Portella d'en Serra....24
 Puig des Molins....27–8
 Sa Penya..................19
 Sa Peixateria
 (fish market)...........20
 Sa Torre...................19
 Teatro Pereira...........27
El Pilar.......................58
El Rincón del Marino
 (Bol Nou)................34
environment............7–8
Es Caló de
 Sant Agustí.............57
Es Canar.....................51
Es Castellar rocks........40
Es Cavallet beach........32
Es Corb Marí..........31–2
Es Cubells..................35
Es Cuiram..................48
Es Mal Pas beach........57
Es Pou d'es Lleò.........52
Es Pujols....................56
Es Vedrà................35–6
Església de Nostra Mare
 de Deu de Jésus........50
Església
 de Sant Miquel.........43
Església
 es Puig de Missa.......51
Estany des Peix...........54
Estany Pudent.............54

Far de la Mola.........57–8
festivals.................62–3
Finca (farmhouse)
 holidays...................77
Formentera..............53–9

Geography...............5–7
golf...........................69

Hiking.......................69
history...................12–13
horse-riding...............69
hotels.....................77–9

Jesús.........................50

La Mola......................57
La Savina...................54
language....................10
Las Dalias restaurant...52

Macabich, Isidor.........26
Moli Vell windmill.....58
Museun Etnològic
 d'Eivissa
 i Formentera...........51
music.........................62

Nightlife....................68
nudist beaches............75

Painting.....................61
people....................8–10
Pirata Bus bar.............57
Platja d'en Bossa.........29
Platja de Llevant.........55
Platja de Migjorn.........57
Platja de
 Tramuntana..............57
politics.......................11
Port de Benirrás...........44
Port de Sant Miquel
 de Balansat..............43
Portinatx.....................47
Portitxol.....................44
posters.......................61
Punta Arabi
 hippy market.........51–2
Punta de Sa Torre........47
Punta de
 Ses Torres................45

Restaurants.............66–7
Roca Llisa..................50

Sa Caleta.................33–4
Sa Capella
 de Santa Agnès........40
Sa Talaia
 de Sant Josep............35
Sant Agustí
 d'es Vedrà................37
Sant Antoni
 de Portmany..........40–1
Sant Carles
 de Peralta.................52
Sant Ferran
 de ses Roques...........56
Sant Francesç
 de S'Estany...............30
Sant Francesç Xavier..58
Sant Joan de Labritja...47
Sant Jordi de
 Ses Salines...............30
Sant Josep
 de Sa Talaia...........34–5
Sant Llorenç
 de Balàfia.................46
Sant Mateu
 d'Aubarca...........39, 44
Sant Miquel
 de Balansat..............43
Sant Rafel
 de Sa Creu............38–9
Sant Vicenç
 de sa Cala.................48
Santa Agnès
 de Corona.................39
Santa Eulària
 des Riu..................50–1
Santa Gertrudis
 de Fruitera...............45
S'Espalmador..............55
S'Estufador................58
S'Estanyol..................50
Ses Figuertes..............29
Ses Illetes beach......54–5
Ses Paisses de
 Cala d'Hort..............37
Ses Salines.................31
souvenirs....................74

Talamanca..................49
Tanca d'Allà Dins.......59
Teatro Pereira.............27
Torre de's Garroveret..59
Torre de Sal Rossa......30
Torre d'es Molar.........44
Torre d'es Savinar.......36
Torrent de
 Buscastell.................39
tour operators..............71
tourist information......73
transportation..........71–2

Watersports................69